JEANETTE

M000034272

J *the* oy
$aving *of*

Money Lessons I Learned from my Italian-American
Father & 20 Years as a Consumer Reporter

Real Deal Productions www.JeanettePavini.com

Ordering Information:
For details, contact Jeanette@RealDealDigital.com

Print ISBN: 978-1-09834-177-0

First Edition

For my father, mother, and all those who simply want to create a healthier and more joyous financial life for themselves and their families.

PRAISE FOR *THE JOY OF $AVING*

"Until the day when everyone understands how important it is to have adequate savings on hand, *The Joy of $aving* is a must read. For more than 20 years I've worked with Jeanette Pavini to give consumers the information they need to transform their lives. Whether sounding the alarm on consumer scams, avoiding hidden fees, or sharing secret strategies to stretch your paycheck, Jeanette has been a fierce advocate for consumers everywhere. A worthy recipient of our Consumer Action Consumer Excellence Award, Jeanette's money saving strategies are 'news you can use'!"

Linda Sherry, Director of National Priorities, Consumer Action

"Jeanette Pavini combines her years of Emmy Award-winning consumer reporting skills with a heartfelt understanding of how we all can turn our money worries into a richer and more rewarding way of life – especially during these unexpected and stressful days. *The Joy of $aving* is worth its weight in gold, wit, and wisdom. Buy this book. Then buy one for a friend."

Anne Stanley, personal finance news journalist and editor

"Since the unexpected death of my Marine husband in 2005, who died a week after he returned from his second tour of duty in Iraq, I have called myself an advocate. Unfortunately, even the best advocates need someone to campaign for their cause as well as to help "move" the issue to raise awareness in the public eye. Jeanette Pavini was my avenue to help raise awareness of the injustice affecting military surviving spouse's survival benefit plan, known as the "Widow's Tax", which I worked to repeal.

The Veterans Affairs and Department of Defense benefits for military survivors are overly complex, yet Jeanette's writing style was able to break it down for the typical reader to understand our issue. For example, once I was supposed to be interviewed by a radio station, however, was canceled because the station manager stated that the issue was too confusing. Yet, when Jeanette presented our issue to her viewers and readers, she did so in such an outstanding way that it was clearly understood.

I had the fortunate opportunity on March 6th 2013, to testify before the Joint Senate and House VA Committee hearing. During my testimony, I asked members to refer to Jeanette's video on the USA Today Network and her story in MarketWatch. That year, Gold Star Wives presented an award to Jeanette for her above and beyond support of our Widow's Tax legislative issue. We need more effective journalists like Jeanette!"

Dr. Vivianne Wersel, Gold Star Wives member and advocate

TABLE OF CONTENTS

PROLOGUE

Choosing Joy

In January of 2017 I wasn't feeling very joyful. I had stopped working on a show that I loved being a part of, the reality of my life without my dad had set in, and our country was in a political divide. Some mornings it was pretty tough to get out of bed and put a smile on my face. I decided to go to Spirit Rock in Northern California for a one-day seminar called Awakening Joy. It was led by James Baraz, the author of a book I love, *Awakening Joy: Ten Steps to Happiness*. I am a big fan of his philosophy and practices. As I sat in the audience with about 75 other participants, I asked James how you find joy when it seems like there isn't a lot of joy in your life. He made the point that it was during those moments, that it is most important to try to choose joy and put positive energy out into the world. Wow, I thought, I have a choice here. I know it can be difficult to do, I know it was for me, but when I finally decided to try to choose joy it helped. Having financial struggles is hardly something I would call joyful. But there can be joy in saving money. And it's not just the joy we get from stashing money into our savings account or knowing we paid the best price on our purchase. It's the joy from the sense of empowerment we have when we take action. We can become savvy consumers. So, maybe there isn't joy in your current financial situation, but you can still choose to make your approach to turning things around a joyful one. Joy is a lot of things but I see it as an attitude we can choose.

Maybe it was simpler times, but my parents enjoyed their lives. I think a big part of this joy came from the gratitude they felt. Not to say that my dad wasn't stressed about money while working a full-time job in addition to side work on nights and weekends. But they had grown up and lived for so long by going without, that simply having a roof over their head and food on the table was something to celebrate. Gratitude leads to joy.

Look at today's date. Now picture where you want to be one year from today. Ask yourself, "What would I thank myself for doing today when I look back a year from now?" Imagine for a moment getting excited about calling creditors to lower your interest rates or saving $50 on your grocery bill. As I was thinking of the title for this book, many came to mind. In the end, I felt what this book encompasses is exactly what the title reads: *The Joy of $aving*. It's your money. It's your life. It's your choice. Choose joy. Let's start saving!

INTRODUCTION

"It's not what you make, it's what you save."

This is a *Galdoism*. Galdo Pavini - or as I called him, Dad - had quotes and sayings he lived by. Some he made up; others were words he felt instilled wisdom. And if you were fortunate enough to know him, you heard them quite often. Dad was frugal during an era when being frugal meant you were smart. You weren't cheap, you were savvy. It was a natural side effect of being raised in the Great Depression and living through WWII. As part of the Greatest Generation, my father built a prosperous and fulfilling life while living within his means. The world was at war and his generation faced food shortages, no jobs, and devastated economies. Yet somehow my dad and his peers not only survived, they thrived. We can learn a lot from this generation.

Today we too are faced with serious financial challenges not seen since the Great Depression. The aftermath of a global crisis brings financial anxiety and a feeling of hopelessness. The Greatest Generation faced those same feelings. We can learn from their success by facing our challenges head-on and refusing to give into despair.

Some of the most important lessons my frugal, Italian-American dad modeled for our family were saving something from every paycheck he earned, no matter how meager, and spending less than he earned. While it may seem that the Greatest Generation had it made all along — with inexpensive real estate, free education through the G.I. Bill, and a much lower cost of living, their salaries paled in comparison to what we earn today. You might ask, "How can I save money when I'm struggling to make ends meet?" I am here to assure you that the values and timeless skills my dad used to build a rich and rewarding life will work for you today. They certainly have for me. And whether you're struggling to pay off credit cards, raise your family, drowning in student debt, trying to save to buy your first home, or worrying about retirement, the suggestions in this book can help.

Times have changed, but the basic strategies to successful personal finance are the same. Knowledge is power and power lies within the pages of this book. Pages that lay out a tried-and-true method to get you back on your feet, and if you are already on your feet, the strategy to stand even stronger. Let's put a modern spin on being frugal.

This isn't a book about your 401(k), retirement, or investing. This is a back-to-basics book teaching you simple tactics to save thousands of dollars a year. I will help you help yourself — so you can help others. The bones of this book are the compilation of 20 years of research working as a consumer reporter, more than 10,000 news stories, and thousands of letters from viewers.

The heart of this book beats with the skills I learned from my father. His wise words, life lessons, and humor are woven through these chapters to illustrate that the bedrock of financial security is timeless.

I want to help you go from asking, "Where does all my money go?!" to "Where did all this money come from?!"

You will learn ways to shift your mindset and become empowered by being aware of what you earn, what you spend, and how to save more, all while living a life that you value. The chapter resources and money saving tips covering the major expenses in your monthly budget are designed to support and empower you. You'll be amazed at how many creative solutions there are even when funds are limited. And finally, after helping you help yourself, I'll show you ways to give back without having to spend a dime.

I have an unbelievable story to share about how time and talent can be worth as much or more than money when it comes to giving back. I've found that you can give back, make a difference, and donate significantly without spending a penny of your own cash. By helping yourself, you will be able to help others in your community and beyond. It is a wonderful feeling that money can't buy and it's a value we have been losing sight of as people have to work longer and longer hours to make ends meet.

The Holy Grail

It was during a conversation I had with my father that I discovered the Holy Grail — the secret to saving money. When talking about the feeling we both had the day we got our first paycheck, I was surprised by how vivid his memories were. My 90-year-old father said, "My first paycheck was on June 29, 1942. It was for $3.63." He then proceeded to show me something that finally got me to sit down and write this book. In my father's hands he held a green, leather-bound journal engraved with his initials, GP. As he opened the yellowed pages, I saw a living example of the key to gaining financial freedom. Since that first paycheck in 1942, my father wrote down every penny he earned. On each line of his journal, he kept a log of what he earned that week, the gross, and his take-home pay. Every week for 60 years.

I looked at what he earned the week I was born in May of 1963. His take-home pay that week? He earned $143.22; that month, he earned $572.88! I realize things were far less expensive back in 1963, but c'mon! That check had to provide food, housing, medical, education, clothing, incidentals, gas, electric, insurance, and every other expense that would come while providing for a family of seven.

I was at a loss. How in the world did he do it and with so little income? How did he get to a point where he and my mother could have retired comfortably? The answer lies in that leather-bound book that he kept religiously for decades. He didn't have software or bill pay. He had a journal where he wrote what he earned. In another journal, he wrote his expenses. He divvied his paycheck into envelopes. He had a relationship with cash that we don't seem to have these days. That relationship has been replaced with plastic.

His relationship with cash was the basis for my very first column for MarketWatch. When I was hired to write the *Buyer Beware* column, my editor suggested my first story be about how today's consumer doesn't really have a relationship with cash anymore. We charge or use our debit card for everything. These days we use credit to buy our morning cup of coffee or to put money into our parking meter.

Could there be a reason for our aversion to developing and embracing a relationship with currency?

In fact, there is a reason. As I researched, I found work done by George Lowenstein, a professor of economics and psychology at Carnegie Mellon University, showing that in the moment, people experience more "pain of paying" with cash than with credit cards. That's right, our brains make it far easier and less painful to swipe plastic than it is to turn over our hard-earned cash. Dr. Lowenstein told me that "people may find it less painful to spend with credit cards; but they find it incredibly painful to pay off those cards." My dad was definitely not in emotional pain all those years as he paid for everything with cash. He understood he could be paying interest every time he swiped. Instead, because he knew exactly what he was earning and exactly what he could afford, he was grateful to be able to buy the things he needed to support our family. He was able to avoid debt and save money, which gave him a base of security to build on. As time went on, his savings grew, providing him with peace of mind.

Though I was raised on the envelope system, I'm guilty of not having a relationship with cash myself. Just yesterday I swiped my credit card for two bags of groceries totaling $160 (yikes!). If I had to pay cash, would it have been more difficult to turn over eight $20 bills than it was to swipe a piece of plastic? Would knowing I have a certain amount of cash to spend on groceries make me stick to a budget? Yep! It would have.

"It's not what you make, it's what you save" was my dad's philosophy. And after years of tackling every consumer topic imaginable, news story after news story, I realized something: everything I learned from my 90-year-old father about budgeting and money is 100% right. He had a single mother who couldn't find work, had to accept surplus food from the government, and lived through World War II. The man went from not having 25 cents to buy materials to take a class to become an engineer, to raising five kids in private schools, owning a home in the San Francisco Bay Area, and retiring with money in the bank without ever earning more than $45,000 a year.

Managing money today may be more complex, and it may be harder to use cash – especially currency. But these saving and spending lessons are fundamentally the same as those used by successful people for generations. The challenge is to use technology wisely, and know the tips, tricks, and strategies to use it to our advantage.

I have covered stories highlighting millionaires filing for bankruptcy, and people overextended on credit and not being able to make the total of their minimum payments. I was always trying to find the latest fix to help people dig out of the hole. But what if we just avoid the hole? And if we are in the hole, how to get out and stay out for good. With story after story there was a certain theme to the solution every expert I interviewed would recommend. It was exactly what I had learned growing up. It wasn't rocket science, it was actually quite simple.

Keep track of everything you earn. Save part of every paycheck. Spend what you can afford. Use cash whenever possible. Look for ways other than the obvious to save and earn even more.

My stories started to take a different approach. We all know that there are ways to save money on most purchases. Whether it's using coupons when grocery shopping or getting a multi-policy discount with your insurance company, we know the basic ways to save money. But what I found after 20 years of reporting on consumer topics is that there is always a better way to save. There are always things you can do that will save you even more. And in addition to saving money, there are smart ways that you can even make more money. That's right, you can give yourself a raise.

My passion for writing this book came from reading thousands of letters from viewers. My heart would break reading how a single mom caring for her 11-year-old son with special needs couldn't find any way to get ahead. Or a college graduate, who after a year, couldn't find any work and had no idea how she would start paying her loans back. I have heard the worst of the worst financial situations, scams, and hardships. But it's the everyday struggles of today that affect many of us. Financial stress is a root cause to many personal issues that destroy lives. It is cited as the No. 1 cause of divorce; it can cause severe depression and even suicide. Sixteen million children in this country are hungry every day of their life with their only real meal coming from school lunch. High school graduates are afraid to commit to the price-tag of college, fearing the crushing costs. Parents are faced with the decision of whether to send their child to college or to save for retirement. People feel like they can't get ahead. They have become hopeless. No one wants to live this way. *The Joy of $aving* will help restore your hope and show you that financial security is within your reach.

No matter what your financial situation is, all of us want to pay the least amount of money for the best product or service available. What if I told you the time you spent reading this book could save you thousands of dollars over your lifetime? You can start using these strategies today. No need to open an account or make an investment. All you need to do is take these tips and apply them to your everyday life. Even if you use just one of these tips per chapter, chances are you will be in better financial shape a year from now. You can use the resources provided to help you become a more educated consumer. And in the end, you will feel good about not only helping yourself, but for having the ability to help others. The truth is, you can't afford *not* to read this book.

1. CHANGE YOUR MONEY MINDSET

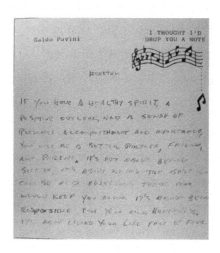

"If you have a healthy spirit, a positive outlook, and a sense of personal accomplishment and importance, you will be a better partner, friend and parent. It's not about being selfish, it's about being the best you can be and rejecting those who would keep you down. It's about being responsible for your own happiness. It's about living your life free of fear."

After my father passed away, I found this written on his stationary tucked away in his desk. This little handwritten note sums up how he handled change and challenge all of his life. It declared his mindset and his goal: living a life free of fear. When it comes to creating a new outlook and approach to our financial health, change is often scary. Many of us are fearful of change, even when changing will make our lives better. It's not unusual.

When I think of my father and mother's lives and the time in history they lived through, I am amazed by their capacity to accept change. Like millions of other young men, on my father's 18th birthday he received his draft notice. Life as he knew it would change and he had no choice but to accept the reality of a world at war. My dad made a conscious choice to be proactive and positive when he was forced to change by events outside his control. When it comes to our money, we, too, can be faced with situations we have no control over, from the sudden loss of a job or a medical emergency, to a pile of credit card bills we can't pay. For my mom and dad, they faced these kinds of challenges by doing the best they could with what they had. Right now, you might be in a similar position, needing to do the best you can despite the circumstances.

When I was struggling with money challenges, one of my biggest fears was that I would never create a career that I truly loved. I wanted to break into TV but it's just not that easy to do. I did some research and found I could host my own show on our public access station. I decided to create a 30-minute show called *The Heart of the Bay*. The show highlighted big-hearted people in the Bay Area who were creating small positive changes. I worked on this show as if it was going to air on a network in prime time. That one show led to doing a segment for a show called *Inside City Limits*. I worked for free to learn the ropes, create a video reel, and meet people in the business. From there, I started doing segments for the local NBC station, and then CBS. This work blossomed into a career I love. I really did create this path for my career in my mind before it became a reality. I gave up on the "never going to happen" attitude and chose to start acting as if I was already a TV professional. I let go of my fears: fears of failure and rejection. From the very first time I did a TV segment reporting, even though I wasn't getting paid, I told people I was a reporter. I changed my mindset. Since I still wasn't making money, I decided to tackle that next: the fear of never making or saving money. I worked several odd jobs while breaking into TV reporting. I started making small changes and my financial situation improved dramatically. Eventually, I learned to welcome change enthusiastically rather than shying away from it.

A different kind of change can happen when we vow to change our life's path. We want to create a better version of ourselves. Maybe it was an "Ah-ha" moment or an epiphany of sorts, but we find ourselves with a new openness to change. I saw examples of people's resolve to change first-hand hundreds and hundreds of times as a reporter. Over the years I had the privilege of interviewing scores of people who overcame hardships through changing their mindset. These stories usually started with what seemed like an impossible challenge, but somehow the people I met asked for help, took action, persevered, and adopted changes that led to success. The moral of these stories is that challenges can inspire people to change their outlook and change their lives. The first step was shifting their mindset.

One of the very first stories I did was on The Homeless Prenatal Program based in San Francisco. I interviewed women who, against all odds, found the inner strength to completely change their lives. These women were about to become mothers and they knew they needed help to create a better life. What impressed me most was their willingness to do the work required to break old, powerful habits and replace them with new, healthy ones. The founder, Martha Ryan, believed in everyone who walked through her door. I remember when my cameraman and I were preparing, I saw Martha outside of the office talking to a homeless woman. This woman was clearly not doing well. I watched as Martha focused her total attention on her, listening to her, and encouraging her in a kind and caring way that almost brought tears to my eyes. Later I asked Martha what inspires her to continue her difficult work. She simply said, "Never underestimate the strength of the human spirit and its willingness to change."

Change and Your Brain

But change is hard. I am just as resistant to it as the next guy. This is especially true when it comes to unhealthy habits, the ones practiced over our whole lives that seem like second nature. Many of us aren't even aware of how hard our brains hold onto underlying beliefs that cause us to make the same disappointing choices over and over, even as we resolve to do better time and time again. With each new failed attempt our brains add fuel to the fire of self-defeating ideas like "we just aren't good with money" or that "it's impossible to make ends meet because of x, y, or z." We just give up and don't do anything. These often unconscious negative thought patterns take a toll on not just our finances, but also on our health and happiness. And it doesn't stop there. The negative beliefs spill over, affecting our partners, children, and communities.

Hardwired negative beliefs are stubborn. They developed for a reason, usually as a defense to protect our egos from experiencing old, painful, and scary emotions. But we can learn to sidestep these financial landmines with knowledge and support. *The Joy of $aving* will describe simple ways to change your financial situation. But simple doesn't always mean easy to stick with. Just like with a diet, you might slip sometimes, and forget to write things down, or spend more money than you planned. These slips are to be expected and can even be a sign that real change is happening. They aren't a reason to give up.

Creating a new money mindset is not about going from living paycheck-to-paycheck to expecting a miracle windfall to appear out of nowhere. Small, consistent changes will change your mindset over time in a comfortable way. As your skills, bank account, and financial health expand, you'll find yourself in a position to both accept help from your community and give back. Gradually, you'll find yourself living the financially secure life you are meant to live, using all of your unique gifts to lead a happier and healthier life. Let's take a few pages here to outline the most common challenges you might experience as you implement new behaviors, and some strategies to stay on track.

✓ The Need for Speed: Unrealistic Goals Derail Success

Fast food, miracle diets, lottery winnings; people tend to treasure instant gratification. But believing that we can make big changes overnight could be the most common set-up for failure. We see it every January, when half the population crowds into gyms and signs up for weight loss programs. By February, the crowds have thinned to pre-New Year's levels and many of the people who vowed to lose weight find themselves heavier than when they started. Why is change easier said than done?

One of the biggest reasons is that people set highly unrealistic expectations to change life-long habits instantly as if they are turning a simple switch on or off. When they struggle, they beat themselves up for not succeeding fast. But our brains are not wired to change quickly. While we may want to change with all our heart, when we start to do things differently, our brain resists the uncomfortable new feeling, and we can find the bad habits getting worse than ever. The cycle of failed attempts reinforces the idea that change is impossible. So, it helps to understand that success will take a while and you will enjoy rewards during that time. And when you feel like your cravings to spend money are worse than ever — it could actually be a sign that the new changes are working, not that you are failing.

Negative Thought Patterns: Guilt vs. Shame

A negative mindset can affect every aspect of a person's life. Studies find that negative, unconscious behaviors are complicated and often shrouded in guilt, fear, or regret. Not the best feelings! To that list we will add shame. Shame is different from guilt and can be downright dangerous to our health. While guilt can motivate you to make positive changes, shame can cause us to freeze up and do nothing. Researcher Dr. Brené Brown from the University of Texas writes about the difference between shame and guilt in this blog post:

> "I believe that there is a profound difference between shame and guilt. I believe that guilt is adaptive and helpful – it's holding something we've done or failed to do up against our values and feeling psychological discomfort. I define shame as the intensely painful feeling or experience of believing that we are flawed and therefore unworthy of love and belonging – something we've experienced, done, or failed to do makes us unworthy of connection. I don't believe shame is helpful or productive."

Rather than a motivator, shame is a big barrier to positive change. People who feel shame begin to believe there is something wrong with them, that they are inherently bad, and will never be able to change. These thoughts can lead to depression, making it hard to get things done, sometimes even to the point of paralysis, which feeds the idea that you're a bad person for not accomplishing your goals and that you'll never change. These thoughts are common and understandable, but I want you to put them out of your mind. I'm here to tell you, you have nothing to be ashamed of, so let it go.

Antidotes for Shame

I understand the struggles of wrestling to make changes to my financial life. I struggled myself for many years and was often embarrassed about it. But there is *no* shame in recognizing you have made a mistake and are taking actions to change.

If you find yourself unable to stick to a new financial program, shame could be creating a defeatist, negative attitude. Here are some things you can do when you find yourself feeling stuck.

- **Practice meditation:** Study after study shows that meditation has profound positive effects on the brain and body. Learning Transcendental Meditation (TM) was a game-changer for me. I learned about it from a friend whose story is too good not to share here. In his 20s he was studying to be a classical guitarist while working as a file clerk in the basement of a major hospital. He hated his job and everyone knew it. His guitar teacher suggested learning TM. Within six weeks with twice daily practice, he not only began to appreciate his job, he began helping co-workers. This was noticed by management who promoted him to ER admissions, where he began to watch doctors do their jobs.

He realized he wanted to become a doctor and was soon on his way to medical school and a successful career as a doctor and surgeon.

- **Join a 12-Step Program:** Debtors Anonymous, Business Debtors Anonymous, and Underearners Anonymous are free programs based on the idea that persistent debt and under-earning are addictions. If you find yourself failing despite repeated self-help efforts, these programs might be helpful. They all offer a wealth of information on their websites, so they are valuable resources even if you don't feel your struggles qualify as an addiction. I know people who have gone through these programs and were able to completely change their financial lives around.

- **Forgive yourself:** You may feel angry or resentful for your current situation, but everyone makes mistakes, and everyone has to learn financial lessons one way or another. Give yourself a break as you travel a new road towards financial stability.

- **Slow down:** When we are trying to make big changes, we often overwhelm ourselves with things to do. Pick a few small actions to take each day and reward yourself when you've completed them.

- **Watch out for negative self-talk:** Treat yourself kindly as you begin new behaviors. For example, instead of telling

→ yourself you're stupid, remind yourself you're learning. You're not a failure, you made a mistake, and you're taking the actions needed to correct the mistake.

- **Remember past success:** Everyone has been successful at something. When the negative thoughts come up, remind yourself that you have been successful before, and can do it again.

- **Get support:** Partner up with someone else who is working to change their financial picture, you can cheer each other on. Join a community of like-minded people, like *The Joy of $aving Community.*

- **Educate yourself:** Read articles, blogs, and books about personal finance and saving. You'll feel newfound power with more information.

- **Read inspirational literature:** Reading how others prevailed over financial hardship can be a great motivator.

The only shame involved in changing your habits, as far as I am concerned, is that it's a shame if you don't make the decision to start!

Procrastination

Most of us procrastinate from time to time. A 2018 study by Fidelity Investments found that 75% of respondents admit to procrastinating about financial decisions, such as starting a savings or retirement account, paying off debt, or setting aside an emergency fund. Almost two-thirds of the respondents realize procrastination carries a price tag. 63% of the respondents had lost money as a result of procrastinating- an average of $300 in the most recent year. The way I look at it is if that $300 a year was put into a savings account, the procrastinator would have a minimum of $3,000. And if that $300 a year was invested for ten years, depending on the rate of return, there could be as much as $5,000 sitting in a bank account. And this is just the cost of lost investment opportunities. If you look at the fees and interest procrastinators pay for late bills and putting off things like car maintenance, the costs can be significant.

The study points out that procrastination is also linked to stress and shame, and like other research on procrastination, the advisors have some suggestions on how to get yourself out of this common rut. Here are some of theirs, along with others.

Stop Procrastinating

At the end of the day, the only way to overcome procrastination is to start working on the project you're avoiding. Here are some of the best ways to get the ball rolling.

- **Set a deadline:** A majority of people say a deadline is the only thing that motivates them to take action. Write the deadline on your calendar.

23

- **Start anywhere:** After taking the first step, procrastinators often report the project was not as hard as it seemed when they were avoiding it. Bottom line? Just start!

- **Small steps:** Breaking big projects down into small steps makes the project seem more doable.

- **Start small and write it down:** Being able to accomplish a series of small goals builds confidence as well as resources.

- **Make it automatic:** Setting up automatic payments gives you one less thing to worry about and keeps you current on bills.

- **Set up alerts:** Set notifications for when bills are due, when your bank accounts go under a certain amount, and when something you need to buy goes down in price.

- **Partner up:** Find a friend who has similar goals and set aside a regular time to report to each other on progress.

Accentuate the Positive: Tell Yourself a Different Story

A few years ago, while I was worrying about something and its potential outcome, I had a very enlightening conversation with a friend who lives by his Buddhist practice. After he listened to me go on and on about my worries and concerns, he calmly said, "Okay, but why are you telling yourself that negative story? Why not tell yourself a different, more positive story?" He was right. I shifted the story I was telling myself and looked at it through a new lens. I changed my mindset to consider arriving at the positive outcome I did want to happen, and I immediately felt much lighter and more hopeful. Once you realize you can focus on the positive outcomes you want, rather than the negative outcomes you fear, it will get easier.

We've been talking about the pain and cost a negative mindset has on your pocketbook and your health. But the flip side is, it actually *pays* to develop a positive, optimistic mindset. The effort you put into cultivating optimism will be worth the payoff. A survey done by psychologist Michelle Gielan, Founder of The Institute for Applied Positive Research, found that 62% of optimists exhibit better financial health — nearly seven times greater than pessimists at 9%. Psychologist Michelle Gielan says that people who are optimistic don't take financial challenges personally. The extremely good news, according to Gielan, is that anyone can learn to adopt an optimist's behavior, even if they don't feel optimistic at the moment. Here are some highlights of the study.

- **Small actions have a major impact**: Enough said.

- **Take the taboo out of money**: Optimists are happy to learn new things about money. They seek out information and discuss it with trusted family, friends, and advisors.

- **Seek progress, not perfection**: Optimists have the courage to try, even if they only have a rough financial plan in place. They value making progress towards a goal. Research shows that making progress and celebrating small milestones leads to a higher success rate.

- **Expect the unexpected:** Optimists experience financial setbacks like everyone else does, and they reported an average of four setbacks in their lives, up to the date of the study. Optimists viewed their setbacks as *setbacks*, not *failures*, and they learned from the experience.

While not all wealthy people are optimists, optimists are more likely to feel confidence around their financial life.

Change Your Money Mindset by Acting 'As if'

In addition to a positive attitude, there are other mindsets and habits that financially successful people tend to follow. These so-called rules may or may not make sense to you at this point, but keeping them in mind will help support you during the transition.

- **Money is a tool, make it work:** Every dollar you invest rather than spend can earn more dollars in income for you. Galdo lived by this rule!

- **Educate yourself:** Find ways to absorb information about money, savings, and investments. Talk about money with people who are successful.

- **Clarity:** Successful personal finance requires tracking, spending, and saving.

- **Goals:** Setting goals is crucial for success. If this is new to you, set small, achievable goals and write them down to build confidence.

- **Challenges happen:** Accept the fact that you cannot control most of what happens in the economy. Sometimes financial life is difficult and you might make mistakes. It happens to everyone and is no reason to abandon your goals.

- **Small changes can yield big results:** Don't let yourself down by expecting big changes fast. Start a savings account, no matter the amount, and add to it consistently. Try not to incur more unsecured debt as you start to make your money work for you.

At this point, the most important thing I can tell you is to get started and keep at it. You can do it! Let's move on to keeping track of your money and start saving now.

Resources

Dr. Brené Brown is a research professor at the University of Houston where she holds the Huffington Foundation Brené Brown Endowed Chair at The Graduate College of Social Work. She has spent the past two decades studying courage, vulnerability, shame, and empathy and is the author of five No. 1 *New York Times* bestsellers: *The Gifts of Imperfection, Daring Greatly, Rising Strong, Braving the Wilderness,* and her latest book, *Dare to Lead.*

Michelle Gielan has spent the past decade researching the link between happiness and success. She is the bestselling author of *Broadcasting Happiness: The Science of Igniting and Sustaining Positive Change* and was named one of the Top 10 authors on resilience by the *Harvard Business Review*. You can read more about her work at MichelleGielan.com.

Opt for Optimism: Sponsored by Frost Bank, the site is a resource to learn about optimism and help improve financial health.

Transcendental Meditation: Transcendental Meditation is my preferred meditation practice. Their website will give introductory information and tell you how to begin a course. There are numerous other meditation practices available online. Different practices work for different people, so search around to find one that feels right to you.

Ten Percent Happier with Dan Harris, ABC News: Podcast

2. SAVING WILL SAVE YOU

Bouncing Back to Basics

"In my day you would earn a quarter, spend twenty cents and save a nickel. Your generation spends the quarter and then borrows another quarter at 25% interest."

This was one of my father's famous "Galdoisms" and as usual, he was right. I heard him say this often when I was in my early 20s, because I was borrowing many quarters and paying the expensive, sneaky interest. I was automatically reaching for a credit card whenever I didn't have cash to buy things I thought I needed. I wasn't really thinking about what would happen when that bill showed up in my mailbox a few weeks down the road. At one point, I was so crushed with credit card debt, I felt like I would never get out from under it. In fact, it can and often does take years to pay off your balances if you are only focused on making the minimum payment. In 2019, the average credit card debt was $6,194. Let's say the interest on your credit card is 18%. If you were to make a minimum payment of the interest plus 1% of the balance, you would be paying a monthly payment of $154.85. It would take you over 24 years to pay that debt off. Additionally, that $6,194 would end up costing you $8,714.05 in interest for a grand total of $14,908.05. Credit cards can be a very expensive habit.

Now there are emergencies that do come along and you may have to use a credit card. That is okay and really what they should be used for. We'll have more on digging out of debt later on in this chapter. Right now, we're focusing on saving.

My dad did use a credit card occasionally, but only when he knew he could pay the balance in full when it came due. To say he did not believe in paying someone else interest and fees is an understatement. "If money comes out of your right pocket and you're not putting it in your left pocket, you're putting it in somebody's else's pocket," he told me during a segment we did for Hallmark's Home & Family Show. He didn't want his money to end up in anyone else's pocket for no reason, and neither should you.

But it was the part about saving the nickel that always got me. How was my dad able to save money on his blue-collar salary with seven people to feed and clothe? The answer: *saving was as important* as *spending* to him.

"We came out of the Depression and you saved whatever money you could. Saved whatever food you could. You wouldn't waste anything," he told me often.

Now you might say that was then, this is now, and there is no way I can save any amount of money in this economy. Or you might believe that you cannot save as long as you have high-interest credit card debt to pay. And many, many Americans would agree with you. According to a 2019 Bankrate survey, only 18% of Americans report they could live off their savings for six months. In fact, almost 70% say they have less than a $1,000 cushion and nearly 40% would need to borrow money to cover a $1,000 emergency. Clearly, Americans are not the best savers. Additionally, according to the 2019 annual survey by GOBankingRates.com, even during the times of nearly full employment and a robust economy, close to half of people have zero dollars in a savings account. It's hard to believe, but in fact, by *not* creating a savings account, you could be setting the stage for a vicious cycle of revolving debt. Believe me, I understand the challenges of saving when you feel you are scraping by each month. Even though I learned the value of saving money from my parents, I couldn't find a way to develop that practice for years.

The psychological stress of not having enough money is well- known. But debt can also take a toll on physical health. A 2010 analysis of more than 60 research papers by the National Institutes of Health found that unmanageable debt is associated with higher stress, depression, sleep disorders, substance abuse, and obesity. Tragically, the studies confirm that there is a correlation between debt and suicide.

I, too, used to think I could put a saving and spending plan on hold until later. The fact is, without a savings account, you are virtually guaranteeing you will need to borrow money at some point. Think about it. Appliances wear out. Cars need brake jobs, tires, and other maintenance. It's not a question of if, it's a matter of when. By having a plan and money in a savings account, you avoid reaching for the credit card, and going into debt.

Savings provide us with so much more than money in the bank. A 2014 study by the Northwestern Mutual Insurance Company found that saving is linked to increased happiness. People who are "planners" set goals and take steps to do things like saving money. The act of achieving their goals helps them feel happier and more positive about their lives when compared to people who do not plan. On a related note, Consumer Federation of America found a strong relationship between having spending and saving plans and maintaining emergency funds, particularly for low-income individuals.

Personally, I found that creating spending and saving plans that support me to be one of my proudest accomplishments, and I'm sure you will too. Knowing you can take care of yourself financially provides a sense of power and security.

If you find yourself without savings, it's okay. Don't dwell on the past or what you could have done differently. It doesn't matter. You have a choice right now to start where you are and find new ways to approach your personal finances. What you start doing today is what matters. And trust me, we'll show you how small changes can add up to big savings, once you understand what your spending habits are. ✓

Awareness: Why Tracking is the Key to Taking Control

I recently had a long conversation with an old friend. In between catching-up on our kids and the economy, we found ourselves deep in a conversation about our monthly budgets. We both wondered exactly where our money was going. We made a deal: we would both take a look at every monthly expense we have, write it down, and reconnect in one week. Taking a deep dive into your monthly expenses can seem like a daunting task, and many of us don't start because we're afraid of what we'll find. It's understandable to feel that way, but I've found time and time again that once I get started, jotting down the numbers is easier than I expected.

Financial uncertainty has been a source of fear and insecurity for generations. And when the economy takes a hit due to things beyond our control, it's important to understand exactly where you stand. In the past year, the world has experienced unimaginable losses. Unemployment is at an all-time high. Small businesses are struggling and many are failing. Maybe you feel paralyzed. We talked about the costs of procrastination and paralysis in Chapter 1, and how it pays to get started, no matter what. Here are a few simple steps to taking control of your expenses, instead of your expenses taking control of you.

- **Fixed expenses:** Take inventory of every fixed monthly expense you have and make a list. Expenses such as your mortgage, rent, or your monthly cellphone bill are usually set in stone or relatively close in cost each month.

- **Flexible expenses:** Other expenses may vary such as groceries, wardrobe, and gas. I call these your "flexible expenses." Take a good educated guess on what you spend in those categories. Think of everything you spend money on. If you want to be really exact, track in a notebook every dollar you spend for a month. This way you don't overlook things like coffee or meal deliveries. This category is where you will be able to garner the most savings. We'll be telling you literally hundreds of ways to save on these expenses throughout the book.

- **Recurring expenses:** Take any semi-annual or annual payments you make for something and calculate what that breaks down to on a monthly basis.

- **Examine credit cards:** Look at your charge card statements very closely. I find we not only pull out and use our credit cards unconsciously, but we also pay the bills unconsciously. Look for any recurring charges and decide if they are really necessary. A few years ago, I did this and found over $100 a month on recurring charges for things I could do without. Make the call and set up the cancelation. Don't procrastinate. Just pick up the phone or go online and cancel.

- **Interest:** Determine how much money you are paying monthly in interest and fees for your credit cards, car payments, and any other loan or debt. While you're at it, review any questionable charges and fees. If you find one, dispute it.

These five steps are the key to the knowledge you need to take control. You can't see where the leaks are if you aren't aware what's coming in and what's going out. You need a good tracking system that feels easy for you to use. My dad used his little notebook religiously and paired it with envelopes that held the weekly allotments. This might work for you, too. But if pen and paper aren't for you, there are a number of great alternatives. It's worth doing some research to find a system you like.

Tracking Systems: The Envelope System

My dad paired his trusty notebook with the very basic envelope system. My parents literally used categorized envelopes to make sure they stayed within their monthly budget. My dad would cash his paycheck and he divided the money between white envelopes marked groceries, gas, personal care, and so on. He also had an envelope for savings. Regardless of what he earned, my dad would always pay himself *first* by saving something from every check. Even if it was just a few dollars. And when an envelope ran out of money, it wasn't replenished until the next payday. This basic system guaranteed they lived within their means, planned their weekly spending, and grew their savings. My dad would always say, if he got down to the last few dollars in the grocery envelope, we'd be eating a lotta pasta. The notebook and envelopes were the basis of my dad's relationship with money. Holding cash in his hands, he had a visual and physical sense of that money and its value. He could see the money going in and going out. And as I reported in that early column I wrote, when we use cash rather than credit cards, we spend less money.

Modern conveniences like electronic deposits and autopay can muddy the waters about the reality of what we can afford and disconnect us from our cash. I suggest as you transition to this new way of keeping track of spending, you experiment with both electronics and envelopes. I would bet just about anything that if you were to put $150 cash a week away for groceries, you would not overspend at the market. You would have that cash, buy what's on sale, use coupons, and stretch your dollar. You can also accomplish the same goal by using a debit card. If you just pull out a credit card, it is far easier to overspend.

We proved this fact first-hand at CBS in San Francisco with a series called *Becoming a Millionaire*. Every night we highlighted ways to set goals and track expenses, following people who were trying the exercises for the first time. Every person reported that the tracking exercises were eye-opening. They gained valuable insight into how their money mindset was holding them back, and they never would have realized it without tracking all their expenses and writing down their goals.

It's important to note that there is a difference between cash and currency. Currency, of course, is the paper dollar bills of any denomination. Cash, rather, really refers to the liquid asset. Paying with a debit card or a check or a bank transfer from your checking or savings accounts – technically, these are all cash payments, too. It's nice when you can use currency for certain expenses, although fewer businesses like to take currency these days. But the crucial difference is between cash and credit. And the crucial lesson is to form the habit of paying in cash and only using credit cards when truly needed.

While my dad used the old-school methods, there could be many reasons you might feel more comfortable using something different. If you don't want to have that much cash in your house, a debit card with a check register can take the place of cash. Luckily, there are plenty of tracking systems available. Let's take a look at some of the most popular ones.

A Virtual Envelope

There is a modern-day version of the envelope system. It is the same in theory as dad's version, and anything that helps us become more accountable, is a step in the right direction. Here are some of the best envelope budgeting apps for Android & iOS.

- Goodbudget: Budget and finance app that includes great financial education and resources

- 1Money: Expense tracker, money manager, budget

- Fudget: Budget and expense tracking app

- Wallet: Finance tracker and budget planner

- Vault: Budget planner

- Monefy: Money manager

- **Free templates:** Search online for free personal finance templates. There are hundreds of options for electronic devices. Take some time to see which ones are best for your needs. If you work in a traditional job that pays you regularly, you might prefer a different system than someone who has multiple income streams. And pay attention to the layout. If you react better to charts and graphs than lists of numbers, you can find a template that's better for you. Microsoft Excel, Apple Numbers, and Google Sheets all have free annual budget templates that you can customize and make your own. The upside to these is that they are private but you will need to manually add the information from other sources.

- **Free software and apps:** I have done many stories on Mint.com. It's free. It is owned by Intuit and offers ways to help understand your current financial situation and plan for the future. Like other online apps, it syncs with your accounts to record your spending and saving habits in real time. Another free option you might like is Goodbudget.com which is based on the envelope system and offers online courses to help you set up your own budget.

- **Lower cost software and apps:** The majority of personal finance software and apps charge a monthly or annual fee. Apps are designed with different goals in mind. If your goal is paying off debt, you might want to check out youneedabudget.com. Known by its community as YNAB, the app has a dedicated following and works on a zero-based budgeting system, where you assign a category to every dollar you earn. Mvelopes.com uses a virtual envelope system to assign value to all of your earnings. There are many, many more apps out there. Almost all offer free trial periods for the first month or so, and I suggest trying before buying in this case.

Once you track your spending for a few months, you'll get a sense of your habits. Most of us have areas where we can make simple changes that will free up cash for our savings accounts. In addition to an emergency fund, there are other savings accounts financially secure people need, including retirement accounts. Here are some ways to pump up the volume on savings.

A Must-Have: Emergency Funds

If you don't save for a rainy day, (how much rainier does it get than a global pandemic and recession?) the day will come when you won't be able to pay for an emergency. And the question is not *if* there will be an emergency, but *when*. That emergency might be an unexpected car repair, expensive medical bills, or a sudden job loss.

Research done by The Urban Institute in 2016 found a shocking fact: Even a small cash cushion can help people survive hard times. As little as $250 can significantly reduce the risk that a family will miss paying a utility bill or be evicted. And savings can be at least as important as income. The study found low-income families with savings of between $2,000 and

$4,999 are more financially resilient than middle-income families earning far more and who do not save.

Ideally, your emergency fund should contain enough money to cover three to six months of expenses. The Bureau of Labor and Statistics estimates average yearly household spending at around $5,000 per month. That's a hefty emergency fund to put together, but it can be done, and many people find that once they stop wasting money on things they don't really need or use, they can build reserves without stress.

The most important thing about saving is to start now, even if you think it's impossible to make ends meet. You might ask how you can save money when you already have debt that charges interest. It seems counterintuitive, but by following the strategies and tips in this book you can lower your monthly costs and in turn put that money into a savings. Saving money can become a learned habit.

Don't Be a Debt Slave, Learn to Save

One evening my husband was reminiscing of how as a young boy he would save every penny he earned from his newspaper route and shoveling snow. And when he had saved a few dollars, he would proudly walk to the bank, savings passbook in hand, and deposit that cash into his account. It gave me such a warm feeling and memory of my days as a child. I would sweep people's sidewalks and do odd jobs to earn extra money to add to my 15 cents-a-week allowance. When I saved $5, I would have such pride walking into our neighborhood bank and watching the teller write in the amount and stamp my passbook. The system of banking has certainly changed, but the pride one feels when saving money, no matter the amount, hasn't. As we continued the conversation, we both had a bit of an epiphany. We realized we had been taught from a very young age to value every penny and the importance of having savings. His parents also lived through the Depression and the war. We admitted that this lesson in saving was not something we necessarily instilled in our own children, at least not to the extent that it was instilled in us.

In addition to all of the money saving tips included in this book, here are a few strategies to bump up your savings account:

- **Save windfalls:** All or a portion of windfalls from tax returns or other unexpected cash infusions can go straight into savings.

- **Save change:** You'll be surprised how nickels and dimes add up. I brought my change to a coin-counting kiosk and walked out with $62.

- **Spending moratoriums:** Set up regular "no-shopping" days.

- **Save one income:** For partners who are able to lower their expenses, they might be able to bank one of their incomes, or a portion of it.

- **Automatic pay:** Have your bank automatically withdraw money from each paycheck into a savings account.

- **Side gigs:** If you are trying to save money for something specific, an extra job might help. Just remember it's not healthy to work around the clock.

So, while we love saving money on purchases, we also love saving a portion of our earnings for emergencies and retirement. Make it fun. About 20 years ago, I started an automatic withdrawal from my checking into my savings. I transferred $50 every two weeks from my paycheck. I just recently transferred that money and it really added up: I had close to $25,000.

When you are about to make a purchase and are on the fence, wait. Then ask yourself: What would I rather have: this item or more money in the bank? If you are still on the fence, put the item on hold for 24 hours. Chances are the impulse to buy will be gone and the money will be saved.

When I was in my early 20s and overwhelmed with debt, I decided to get a night and weekend job as a cocktail waitress with the goal to work until the credit card debt was paid off. I reached my goal within a couple of months. It may take you six weeks; it may take you six months. But picking up some extra work with the sole purpose to pay off debt may be a good solution. While you are working to pay off the debt, you can also start your savings habit. Take a portion of this new income and automatically put it into a savings account, too. Once the credit cards are paid off, take the money you would use monthly to pay off your debt and put it into your savings. The important thing is to start the new habit of saving something. Even if it is $5 a week, you will have that $260 in an account by the end of the year.

Frugality is now gaining popularity, and while it might not be trendy yet, it will never go out of style.

How Can I Save When I Have Credit Card Debt?

Many of us still owe money to creditors and are paying interest on those balances. It's extremely important that you don't put your head in the sand about obligations to pay off that debt. If you are struggling to make minimum payments every month, there are organizations that can help.

When I was reporting with CBS in San Francisco, I would turn to Consumer Credit Counseling Service (CCCS) as the experts for stories I was covering on debt. In fact, one evening we set up a live phone bank during the evening newscasts. Viewers called in to speak with a CCCS counselor. The phones were ringing off the hook! In fact, we kept going past 7 p.m. CCCS is a nonprofit helping people with budgeting assistance, financial education, and developing a debt management plan. They can often negotiate lower interest rates on your cards and can help you consolidate the loans into a single payment. It's extremely important that you check with the Better Business Bureau about any debt consolidation service you use. There are unscrupulous players in the field who take money from consumers and don't pay off the debts.

Also be careful while you are paying off debt that you avoid taking on more debt at the same time. There are many people who dig out of debt only to find themselves back in the same position once they start using credit cards again.

It's true that you will save money on interest if you pay debts off quickly. However, if you pay debts off quickly at the expense of creating a savings account, the chances are you will wind up at debt's door again and again.

Helping Others

This is a simple way to help your own inner circle. Once you have mastered your own monthly budget, help a friend or family member to do the same. Giving a few hours of your time to help guide others can make a significant difference in their lives.

Resources

Consumer Federation of America: The Consumer Federation of America (CFA) is an association of non-profit consumer organizations that was established in 1968 to advance consumer interest through research, advocacy, and education. Today, more than 250 of these groups participate in the federation and govern it through their representatives on the organization's Board of Directors. CFA is a research, advocacy, education, and service organization.

Consumer Credit Counseling Services (CCCS): Consumer credit counseling service agencies are nonprofit organizations that will help you find a workable solution to financial problems.

Each CCCS agency offers a common set of services, including financial education, budgeting assistance, and debt management plans.

Be very skeptical of any consumer service that claims it will solve your debt problems for pennies on the dollar. Often these are for-profit organizations which will charge you for services that are otherwise free. In worst-case scenarios, they are scams and you will lose money you think is going to your creditors.

3. GIVE YOURSELF A RAISE

Over my career, I have done several stories that received an overwhelming response from viewers. After an appearance on the *Today Show* where I showed viewers ways to earn extra money by finding "moonlighting jobs" such as being a taste-tester, mystery shopper, or a mock juror, I received an email from the producer. She said, "This segment is a web sensation" and this web sensation was one of the top stories of the day. I was so excited. Not only was the story a success, but the information shared might help people who were looking for ways to make extra money. And when I did a TV segment and an article on how to give yourself a $6,000-a-year raise, I received heart-breaking, grateful emails from people who were barely making ends meet, and were encouraged to try these tips to keep more money in their pocket. I recall one letter in particular from a woman in Washington who had $65 a month in disposable income. The common thread to the thousands of letters I have received is that people want to increase their income, but most people live paycheck-to-paycheck without a cost-of-living increase in sight. When the economy nosedives, so do our finances if we haven't saved or set aside emergency funds. In addition to the chapters in this book that target specific areas of our monthly expenses, here we will discover additional ways to save and earn extra money. Let's start with giving yourself a raise and then we will go onto making some Moonlighting Money.

Giving Yourself That Raise

Think of a time when you received a pay raise. It used to be that every year you would usually get a small increase in your pay. But these days our cost-of-living increases are not guaranteed. Let's say you earn $60,000 a year and you receive a 3% raise. That would give you an extra $150 a month, maybe $100 after taxes. What a pay raise boils down to is one thing: more money in your pocket. The truth, as I see it, is that every expense you cut out or cut back on gives you the same result: more money in your pocket. Let's say you can shave $8,000 a year off of your expenses. That's the equivalent of giving yourself about a $12,000 a year raise before taxes. And if you follow these tips, you may find you can earn much more than a typical pay raise.

Grocery Shopping

We go into greater detail in the chapter called Slash Your Grocery Bill, but since groceries are one area you can really cutback on, I felt we should also mention it here. The average family of four spends between $1,111.70 and $1,301.10 a month on groceries according to the USDA. That is as much as $15,612 a year. I also reported on many families who spend double that amount. But you could slash your grocery bill by at least 35% and as much as 50% by doing these four simple things.

- Build your weekly menu around what is on sale at your grocery store. You will find the weekly deals in the paper flyers that come in the mail or you can look online. Sales usually start on Wednesdays.

- If you do nothing else: Join your grocery store's loyalty programs. They should be free and they provide added sales and perks at check-out.

- Use coupons to add to your savings. Find them online, in newspapers, magazines, apps, and your favorite products' website. And remember, coupons are like free money. You might think coupons only come in paper form, but many stores and pharmacies offer e-coupons applied to your loyalty card.

- If a sale item you want is out of stock, ask for a raincheck. This means when the item comes back in stock, you will get it at the sale price. I have saved thousands of dollars over the years by doing this.

By making these changes to your grocery shopping routine and lowering your grocery bill by 35%, you can save between $4,670 and $5,464 a year.

Brown Bag It

Now that you have the grocery shopping savings strategies in play, you can take things one step further. When I was growing up, we brought a bag lunch every day to school. Even my dad brought his brown bag lunch to work. We also had to bring our brown paper bags home to reuse them. By packing your own lunch, you can save thousands (Yes, thousands) of dollars off of your yearly food expenses. And I would bet, if you pick up the right ingredients, you can make a sandwich just as good as a deli.

Here's an example from a news story I did a few years ago: The average deli sandwich with turkey and cheese, a bag of chips, a cookie, and iced tea will cost you about $11.50 a day. That is close to $3,000 annually, just for lunch for one person. You can create that same lunch at home for about $2.53 a day, or about $658 a year. When buying your groceries for lunch, use the same money saving strategies you use for grocery shopping: Plan your menu around what is on sale, join loyalty clubs, use coupons, and ask for rainchecks. Depending on what you spend when buying lunch, you can save about $2,332 per person a year.

Skip the Scones and Coffee

The same mindset and strategies apply to your morning cup of coffee, breakfast, and snack. Here is where it is very easy to unconsciously overspend. Let's say you spend an average of $2.10 on your morning cup of coffee (more if it's a latte) five days a week. That's about $546 a year. Now add to that a scone or muffin for $3, so another $780 annually. By making your own coffee and bringing a snack from home you can save about $800 a year. You can easily buy coffee beans from popular coffee chains and make your own for a fraction of the cost.

As you can see, adjusting our mindset and habits when it comes to spending money on food can make a significant difference in our annual budget. Take a few minutes to do the proper planning and prepping. Think of it as an investment of your time. By making these changes to your grocery shopping, bringing a brown bag lunch, and skipping the coffee shop, based on national averages a family of four could save over $10,000 a year, which is like earning $15,000 or more depending on your tax bracket. If you think of it in these terms, it's worth the time it takes to apply these strategies to your life.

Now that we can check groceries off the list, let's move onto other ways to give yourself that raise.

Do-it-Yourself Dry Cleaning

Many consumers use at-home dry cleaning kits and save the professional dry cleaners for special garments. A $10 kit will cover four loads which equates to about 16 items. On average, you can save several hundreds of dollars a year depending on how much you use your dry cleaner.

Gym Memberships

If you are like me, you have enthusiastically joined gyms only to end up going once or twice a month. When this happens, those workouts end up costing quite a bit. A typical gym membership costs between $40 and $55 a month, some are in the hundreds. One way to cut the cost is streaming your workouts online or, better yet, see if any workout shows are included with your cable package. You can also switch to a no-frills gym. If you want a gym experience, consider your local community college. Many offer inexpensive membership access to their facilities and swimming pools. Depending on what you are currently paying at your gym, you could save $600 a year by making a switch.

Online Shopping

Do not make any online purchase without checking for a coupon or promo code. It only takes a minute to do and the potential savings will be well worth your time. You can find thousands of coupon codes on everything from travel and wine to clothing and sports gear. The easiest way to find coupons is to do a quick search for coupon or promo codes.

When making a purchase, whether online or in the store, ask what their price adjustment policy is. This means if the items you purchase go down in price within a certain period of time (usually 14 days) the store will give you back the difference between what you paid and the new sale price. So, if you paid $100 for clothes and 10 days later those same clothes were on sale for $60, you would get $40 back. I have saved thousands of dollars over my lifetime doing this one simple thing. Most major department stores and chains offer some type of a price adjustment. And usually you do not need to bring back the items, just the receipt.

Gas Up

Go an extra mile (or two) to save a little cash on gas. By using a gasoline price comparison app like GasBuddy, you can find the cheapest gas in town. If you belong to a warehouse club, you might find the best prices through them. Through some grocery stores, you can put in your loyalty club number and receive an additional savings at the gas pump.

This next tip saved me a lot of money while I was commuting to work. When I was first working at CBS San Francisco, I would drive into the city. It was about 60 miles a day roundtrip. Between what I paid for gas and parking in the City, I was spending about $450 a month. I decided to try the train and I loved it. Not only was I saving about $350 but I was able to take advantage of commuter tax benefits. If you use public transportation to commute, be sure to see if you qualify for the tax benefits. Another perk: you're hands-free so you can use this time to get a head start on work, read a book, or my favorite, meditate. If you are living in a two-driver household and taking separate cars, downsizing to one car can save you thousands of dollars a year between car payments, maintenance, insurance, gas, and parking.

Get Credit for Using Credit

I am not a fan of using credit cards unless you can pay the balance off by the due date. You also should make sure you truly need to make the purchase. If you are able to pay off the balances, you can make credit cards work to your advantage. Most cards reward their users with points. And these points can be used for cash back, travel, gift cards, and more. Reassess your credit cards and make sure you are using a card that is generous with their rewards. Some credit cards will offer double or triple points in certain categories. For example, you may get double points when you buy groceries or triple at gas stations. Reward programs vary, so make sure you read all of the rules. When I met my husband, he had been using the same card for years. I asked him if he was taking advantage of the cashback option. He hadn't been and we decided to check. He had several hundred dollars just sitting there waiting to be cashed in. (I scored some points of my own on that one.)

If you are using a credit card to make an electronics purchase, your card may offer an extended warranty at no additional charge. This saved me once when I damaged a phone and my credit card covered it.

Unclaimed Property

When certain checks are sent to you, such as an insurance or government payment, and if for some reason you do not receive it, those payments go into a government system called Unclaimed Property. To find out if you have any unclaimed funds, just search "Unclaimed Property" and the state you live in. I found that I had an insurance refund of about $80 waiting for me. The most I found was $300 for a friend of mine. It is really simple to use and the response is immediate. But do be careful to use only the official state programs. There is no fee to search for and claim your unclaimed property — if you use your official state program. Each state has laws and unclaimed property programs that make this service available to its citizens. Check first with the National Association of Unclaimed Property Administrators.

The organization, a Network of the National Association of State Treasurers, notes that there are third-party "finders" that may offer to locate and claim your unclaimed property for a fee. While not required to obtain your unclaimed property, these third-party services are in most cases legal. But why give someone else the money that belongs to you? Good luck!

One Extra Mortgage Payment

This is a tip that will save you money over time and, in the long run, if you plan to live in your home for a long time. Possibly by saving in other areas of your budget, you can apply some of that money to your mortgage principal. Check with your lender on how much money you would save by making one extra mortgage payment a year. When I did a story on this a few years ago, an extra payment on an average 30-year mortgage could shave as much as seven years off the life of the mortgage and save many thousands of dollars. You need to check with your lender to make sure the extra payment goes directly to principal.

If you follow even some of these savings strategies, you are not only giving yourself the equivalent of a significant raise, but you are taking control of your personal finances. Use some of these strategies or all of them: try them daily or twice a week.

The more you follow them, the more you save. Now let's get started on more ways to earn some extra cash.

Moonlighting Money

Imagine for a minute actually getting paid to eat chocolate, go shopping, or even to dine at a high-end restaurant. More and more companies are paying people for their opinions on everything from potato chips to computer chips and everything in between. It's called "moonlighting money" and it's a great way to earn a few extra dollars while having fun.

In 2019, 13 million Americans picked up extra jobs and sought outside work. With the recent jump in unemployment, I would bet these numbers will continue to rise. I have done this story several times and it always gets an overwhelming response. I think it is because some of these jobs don't feel like work at all. Often, before companies bring a product to market, they want opinions about it from real people. And work in a focus group will pay you far more than a penny for your thoughts. You can get paid to eat, drink, and be merry. Keep in mind, most of these side gigs are sporadic and some are seasonal. You won't be able to earn a living doing these. But it is a way to earn some extra money and some jobs you can do from home.

Focus Groups

These groups do everything from taste-testing to rating product packaging. Search for market research companies in your area and sign up in their database. You can make $40 to

$75 for 45 minutes... and up to a couple hundred for the day depending on the work. If you are a professional in a field, such as a nurse or doctor, you can get paid much more. These companies take it very seriously and in some cases the participants cannot even see the others in the study (so they can't gauge their opinions by others' reactions). In-person groups usually get paid more than online surveys. Parents are often called upon for their opinions. The day I went to a focus group to interview participants, they were taste testing granola, milk shakes, and chocolate. They were there about an hour and left with $75 cash. Because of the pandemic many focus groups are now virtual, so you may be able to earn extra cash without leaving home.

Mock Juries

Before heading to the courtroom, some attorneys test their cases on a mock jury. These mock trials are done both in person and virtually. The pay can range from $100 to $200. I have sat in during some of these jury opinion groups and it is quite fascinating. Or you can try online at sites like eJury.com which pay $5 to $10 for about 35 minutes of your time.

Mystery Shopper

A variety of businesses, from restaurants to clothing stores, hire mystery shoppers to get an idea of what their customer's experience is like. Many times, in addition to your pay, you get to keep the merchandise. I followed a professional mystery shopper for a day. She had a couple of assignments and then came back to her home and filled out the paperwork.

Online Survey Participant

Take online surveys and then redeem them for online gift cards to websites like Macy's or Amazon, get magazine subscriptions, or a hotel gift card.

Tutor

Other ways to make extra cash is by tutoring especially in a foreign language. And because video conferencing has become the norm these days, you don't even have to leave your home.

Don't Get Scammed!

As with anything, consumers need to be aware of potential scams. Here are some things to pay close attention to.

- **Never pay:** There should never be any fees paid by you for working on focus groups or as a mystery shopper.

- **Beware of certification programs:** Make sure that you know what the certification is for and how you might benefit.

- **No wire transfers:** Never do a wire transfer of money for a mystery shopper job.

- **Research:** Check with the Better Business Bureau before signing up for a mystery shopper or focus group job.

Resources

Unclaimed Property: National Association of Unclaimed Property Administrators

Mysteryshop.org

Check the Federal Trade Commission website for more on mystery shopping (www.ftc.gov)

4. SLASH YOUR GROCERY BILL

Every evening at 5:15, I would hear my mother's voice from the top of our front stairs yelling, "Dinner time!" We would drop our bikes, run inside, wash our hands, and eat. There were seven of us sitting around the table and everything was served family style. I can tell you this, not a morsel of food was ever wasted in our home. Ever! Since both of my parents were products of the Depression and World War II, nothing was left on our plates. They appreciated every ounce of food that made its way into our home and wasting it would be a crime. The other grocery crimes would be not buying groceries on sale and not using coupons. My father would give my mother an envelope with the money set aside for groceries every Friday after payday and mom would grab her envelope with coupons and head to the market.

As a young adult, I tried to follow in my folks' footsteps and pay cash, but more often than not I would slip the credit card out of my wallet to pay my grocery bill. I did notice that when I paid cash, I was so much more aware of what I was buying and what I was spending. I continued to learn new methods for saving money on grocery bills. With the Internet, it's easier than ever to find coupons and codes to stretch your grocery dollars. While out doing news stories across the country, I met so many people faced with the choice of putting food on their table or paying rent. It can be a real struggle to do both. Once you master your grocery spending, you will certainly find that you have money to apply to other expenses and most importantly, put some money into your savings as a cushion for tough times.

As I've mentioned, consumers need to be aware of the *flexible* expenses in our monthly budget, those things that are not set in stone and we can cut back on. Groceries are at the top of that list. These tips will help you slash your monthly grocery bill by up to 50% and get more bang for your buck by making your food last longer.

Grocery Shopping 101

Follow these rules and you'll save money, have a well-stocked pantry, and a well-fed family. Before you get started, you might want to set up a separate email account for newsletters, promotions, and sales. When you sign up for rewards programs and follow brands on social media, you'll be happy to have all the savings information in one place.

- **Sign up for grocery store loyalty/reward programs.** These programs cost you nothing and can be the single best way to save money on groceries. Most larger stores also have an app which will allow you to download savings directly to your phone. It is the most important thing you can do to save money at the grocery store and pharmacies.

- **Plan meals and make a list.** Walking into a grocery store with an empty stomach and no plan can be costly. It may lead to impulse shopping, which could lead to spending more than you should. Set aside a few minutes each week to plan meals based on what's on sale. Check the store's mailed sales circular or website. Try to incorporate ingredients into multiple meals so you don't waste produce, dairy, and other perishables.

- **Coupons:** Find coupons for items on your grocery shopping list to save even more.

- **Shop sales, but read the fine print.** If a sale says five for $10, don't feel obligated to buy all five. Check the store policy. Usually you will get the same discount even if you just buy a single item. The same goes for limits. A sale on frozen dinners might say "limit six." This is a way to keep the item stocked for more customers but it also triggers an impulse in shoppers to buy all six. Only buy what you need.

- **Ask for a rain check.** If you get to the store and the sale item you want is out of stock, ask the store for a rain check. Rain checks are vouchers that entitle you to the sale price whenever the item is back in stock.

- **Read unit prices.** The expiration or best-by date isn't the only must-read when grocery shopping. Unit price is equally as important. On the price tag, you will see a price per ounce (or other unit of measurement). This is the best way to compare prices between brands.

- **Family size is not *always* the best size.** Sometimes family size can really save a bundle. It is common to save $0.50 or more per pound on meat when you buy the bulk packaging. But you can't assume that's the case. You'll need to read unit prices (see above). Sometimes if the regular size is on sale or if you have a coupon it is actually less expensive than the family size.

- **Stock up where you can.** It still pays to stock up even if you only have one or two people living in your home. Stock up on freezer items like meat and bread when they are on sale. Use a permanent marker and write your purchase date on the package so you know how long it's been in the freezer. And remember to rotate the contents of your freezer so that you use what you have.

- **Check expiration dates.** Make sure you'll be able to use perishable items before they expire.

- **Cost of convenience:** Sometimes convenience is worth the extra bucks, but not always. Just about every time something is peeled, cut, or individually packaged, the price goes up. Create your own "convenience" food. As soon as you get home from the store, divvy a box of crackers into individual portions you can throw in lunchboxes. Or take a bag of carrots, peel, and cut them into carrot sticks for an afternoon snack.

- **Find substitutes for expensive items:** If a recipe calls for an expensive liquor you may be able to substitute an extract or fruit concentrate instead. Infused oils can add the flavor of expensive truffles. Search online for other ideas.

Couponing 101

- Gather all the grocery store ads that come in your mail every week.

- Download apps like coupons.com to have coupons loaded directly to your phone. The app also offers cash back offers.

- Organizing coupons will help you remember to use them. Office supply stores have mini accordion files that will fit in a purse. Create categories for food, restaurants, cleaning products, paper goods, personal care, etc. and sort them by expiration date.

- If your coupons won't scan or a cashier is reluctant to accept it, don't be afraid to speak up or ask for a manager. It can also be beneficial to have a store's coupon policy with you when you shop. Some stores do not accept coupons.

- Coupon stacking is combining *different* coupons for the same product. For example, a store coupon along with a printable coupon from a manufacturer website. Combine this with a store sale and now you are saving *three* ways. Not all stores allow coupon stacking, so it is good to familiarize yourself with their coupon policy before you shop.

- Coupon stacking is not to be confused with coupon doubling, which is when a store doubles (or even triples) the value of a single coupon. Usually this is offered as a special store promotion or customer appreciation event. Some stores have a coupon doubling day once a week.

Meat, Poultry, and Seafood Savings

- Befriend your butcher. Ask your butcher when meat, poultry, and seafood is typically marked down, it's usually at the same time every day. Meat is discounted when it's approaching its sell-by date, but it should still be good if you cook it that night or freeze it for later. Just make sure it wasn't previously frozen. Typically, a large cut of meat will be cheaper than the same amount cut into smaller pieces. But some butchers will be happy to cut it up into smaller pieces for free, especially if you're a regular customer.

- Beef is graded and priced for quality; it is judged by the amount of marbling (flecks of fat), color, and maturity. The highest quality is prime, and it's rare to find prime meat at the grocery store. The prime cuts are usually bought by fine restaurants. The next rung down on the beef ladder is choice and below that is select. You can still get a tasty meal with select grade, just be mindful that with less fat you may have to adjust your cooking methods to preserve tenderness.

- Bone-in chicken is typically less expensive (it's that convenience factor again), but a lot of people are intimidated by bones and opt for the more expensive boneless chicken breast. The closer the chicken is to its original form, the less you will pay. Learning how to break down a whole chicken will save you big money over time. To put it into perspective, boneless chicken breast cost nearly $2 more per pound according to the Bureau of Labor Statistics.

- Most seafood has been previously frozen anyway, so unless you live in a coastal community, look past the butcher counter and see if you can save some money buying it from the frozen food aisle.

Produce Aisle Savings

- Stick with seasonal produce. It's easy to forget produce has a season. Thanks to modern technology and speedy shipping, grocers can stock just about anything, any time of year. But it's going to cost you to eat asparagus in fall or berries in winter. Know your produce seasons and shop accordingly.

- Sometimes it's cheaper to buy items like potatoes, tomatoes, avocados, and onions in bags versus individually. For example, I have seen avocados for $2.49 each or $3.99 for a bag of four.

- Consumers tend to undervalue frozen fruits and vegetables. They are frozen at their peak, preserving nutrients which means they can have as much nutritional value as fresh produce. To buy frozen that is comparable to fresh, look at the ingredient list and make the sure the produce is the only item listed, no sauces, seasoning, or syrups added. Here's how buying frozen saves you money:

- If a recipe calls for out-of-season produce, you'll save with frozen.

- You are more likely to find manufacturer coupons for frozen produce, which you can use on top of store sale prices.

- There is no waste when buying frozen, like the stalks on broccoli, which are costing you extra if you are paying by the ounce for fresh produce.

- If you are buying fresh, see if there is a wholesale produce market in your area. Restaurants shop at these markets and the prices can't be beat. The only catch is you have to buy in bulk. Team up with a neighbor to go in on a case of tomatoes or a flat of strawberries.

- Blanch vegetables and they can last between eight and 12 months in a freezer kept at 0° F (-18° C) or below. Blanching preserves vitamins, flavor, and appearance.

Extending the Life of Produce

- **Beware of ethylene.** It's not quite as ominous as it sounds. It's a natural-occurring gas given off in abundance by certain produce, potentially causing quick deterioration and discoloration. Ethylene producers like apples, avocados, bananas, peaches, nectarines, melons, and pears need to be kept separate from other produce so that they don't spoil.

- **Factor in humidity.** Crisper drawers are in just about every refrigerator and for good reason. They control humidity, which is important because produce has a preference. Fruits stay fresher with lower humidity and leafy vegetables with high. As a general rule, keep ethylene emitters that need refrigeration in the lower drawer and those ethylene sensitive veggies in the higher one.

- **Refrain from refrigeration.** Yes, refrigeration extends the shelf life of most produce, but for some foods, you are sacrificing taste and quality. Refrigerated tomatoes may lose flavor and become mealy. Uncut melons belong on the counter where they will best retain flavor and antioxidants. Ripen stone fruits at room temperature or they may never reach perfection. If you've got an abundance of produce, you may need to use more long-term strategies like freezing or canning.

- **Freeze it.** If packaged correctly, fruits and vegetables can last between 8 to 12 months. Blanch vegetables before freezing for optimal flavor, appearance, and nutritional value.

- **Can it.** Home canning is cool again. Use the Ball Pectin Calculator to find the perfect recipe for making your very own jam or jelly. Canned tomato products require special attention to reach a safe acidity level. Some recipes call for lemon juice to boost the acidity but that can alter the flavor, consider substituting every tablespoon of lemon juice with a quarter of a teaspoon of citric acid.

Asparagus

Thickness does not necessarily indicate whether asparagus is tender. Fat and thin stalks can both be delicious, it's a matter of preference. But whichever you choose make sure it is a uniform thickness so it cooks evenly. To determine freshness, look for tightly closed tips.

Berries

Strawberries have a very short shelf life, so when you see stores offering big savings like buy one get one free, make sure you will be able to use them quickly. If they have white or green tips, they were probably picked prematurely.

To make berries and other fruit last longer, don't wash them until you are ready to eat them. Keep the stem on strawberries while you wash, otherwise they may absorb water and lose flavor.

Herbs

You can freeze herbs by chopping them and putting them in ice cube trays with a little water. You can just pop a few out when you need them.

Onions, Potatoes, and Garlic

Don't store them in the fridge. Keep them in a cool, dark, and dry spot. Onions will last even longer if you store them in the legs of a nylon stocking. For this trick, knot the nylon between each onion so they don't touch.

Pears

You will actually get a better quality pear when it's picked early and ripened off the tree. To ripen at home, keep them in a brown paper bag at room temperature. This technique also works for tomatoes and stone fruit like peaches and nectarines.

Salad Greens

Rinse under cold water, drain, and dry in a spinner or colander. Wrap them loosely in a paper towel and place in a sealable plastic bag and then store them in your refrigerator's crisper drawer.

Tomatoes

Most tomatoes are picked early and ripened indoors. These have less flavor than those ripened on the vine. But just because tomatoes are sold on the vine, doesn't necessarily mean they were ripened while still attached to the tomato plant.

Extending the Life of Other Groceries

- The average shelf life of ground spices is about six months, after that they lose their potency. Get in the habit of marking the date you bought a spice on the bottom of the container. This also means spices are one thing you may not want to buy in bulk, be realistic about what you will use. For the highest quality and flavor, purchase whole spices and grind them up as you need them.

- Create less food waste. One of the best ways to stretch grocery dollars is to waste less. I'm not just talking about eating everything in your fridge before it reaches its expiration date. Find ways to use food scraps before they end up in the compost pile. For example, many people know that after roasting a chicken, you should hold onto the bones and trimmings to make chicken stock. Do the same with your vegetables. Veggie waste like carrot peels and broccoli stalks are actually a great way to flavor your broth. Keep a bag in the freezer and load it up till you're ready to make soup.

- Freeze more. Similar to the last tip, this one is all about freezing more so you waste less. Practically anything can be frozen, if stored properly. A vacuum sealer is a great investment if you want to get serious about freezing. FoodSaver estimates you can save up to $2,700 a year when you buy items in bulk, on sale, and prevent waste by freezing food in airtight packages.

Grocery Store Secrets

- Look high and low. Sometimes manufacturers and distributors pay the store to place products at eye level. A lot of times you can find the most inexpensive brands and best deals on the bottom or top of shelves. Look high and low to find store and lesser-known brands.

- Just because an item is on an end aisle, in a special display, or has an oversized price tag, does not mean it's on sale.

- Major brands manufacture their products under different labels. For example, a milk company might manufacture milk and use three different labels. The only differences are the look of the bottle and the price.

Helping Others

Despite the U.S. being one of the most agriculturally rich countries on the planet, hunger is a persistent, serious problem in virtually every state. Millions of children and families face food insecurity every day. In 2018, 14.3 million households had limited or uncertain access to food. Children live in more than

11 million of those households. Many hungry families don't qualify for federal programs.

One simple way to help is to buy extra and donate to your local food bank. Or even easier, donate some of the money you're saving on your grocery bill to an organization that works to end hunger.

If you have more time than money at the moment, local food pantries can often use help. Many operate food rescue programs at local stores or can use a hand with stocking shelves. Anything we can do as individuals to help end hunger can have a lasting impact on people in need.

Today, Feeding America is the nation's largest domestic hunger-relief organization, a powerful and efficient network of food banks across the country. As food insecurity rates hold steady at the highest levels ever, the Feeding America network of food banks has risen to meet the need. They feed 40 million people at risk of hunger, including 12 million children and seven million seniors.

Resources

The National Frozen & Refrigerated Foods Association hosts a series of promotional events, which brands and stores are encouraged to participate in. Knowing what they have planned means you'll know what sales to look out for.

March: National Frozen Food Month, look for best buys on frozen foods.

June: Dairy Month, look for best buys on dairy products.

June/July: Summer Favorites (ice cream and novelties), you'll find bargains these months.

Each year, the Environmental Working Group releases the *Shopper's Guide to Pesticides in Produce.* It includes a list of the Dirty Dozen, the 12 produce items that are most contaminated and the Clean Fifteen, produce with the least pesticides. Use this guide to help determine where you should spend your dollars upgrading to organic.

5. DATE NIGHT

I remember watching my mom get dolled up on Saturday nights once a month. She would put on her best dress, pull out the Aqua Net hairspray, and carefully apply her red lipstick. My dad would put on his nice slacks, dress shirt, topped off with his button-down cardigan. They would get together regularly with five other couples who had been their best friends since 1945. It was one of my parents' date nights and the only cost was for the dish they brought for the potluck. They would rotate houses, enjoy cocktails, and indulge (calorically, not monetarily!) in Italian potluck dinners. After dinner the gals would sit and catch-up while the guys would drink Negronis while playing pinochle around the kitchen table. The lesson learned: It doesn't take money to have a fabulous date night. As I entered adulthood, I found this lesson to be true. Some of my best date nights had nothing to do with where I was, but rather whom I was with. And the most creative nights out were always the most fun. I once did a story called *Dating on a Dime*. There was a couple I followed that had figured out how to enjoy their nights out while staying within a tight budget. They were big into the happy hours and knew how to find the best free concerts. Viewers loved this story as suddenly they realized enjoying time out was once again a possibility.

Date nights and entertainment are usually the first things to go from our budgets when we are tight on money. But it shouldn't be that way. Psychotherapist Gwen Faulkner, M.S.N., Ph.D. feels staying connected is key, regardless of a couple's financial stress or hardship. "One of the most important factors is having caring and supportive relationships within and outside the family, so working to reconnect with your partner and share openly about the stresses you are experiencing is important for the health of the relationship." You can accomplish this reconnection by doing something as simple as taking a walk together. Creating a date to talk and really listen to the other person can be a powerful tool in staying connected.

If you are going through tough times, it is more important than ever to take a break and connect with someone you care about - and just have some fun. With some creativity and proper planning, it's possible to keep both our relationships and wallets happy at the same time. Think back to some of your best dates. It has little to do with the money spent but rather the experience with the people we shared that time with.

You can make date nights easier, less expensive, and more common if you put them on auto-pilot. Pull out your calendar and start researching free and low-cost events for the next few months. Don't forget to check out virtual events. You will find seasonal events at universities, museums, and parks. Both of you mark the dates you're committing to and start planning. Here are some of the best ways to create a date night on a dime. These are just ideas to get you thinking. Some may come, some may go, but there is always a better way to save on a date night.

The Old Standby: Dining Out

On average a dinner for two will cost you between $50 and $60, higher in places like NYC, SF, and Boston. But there are ways to get around high menu prices at your favorite places. It comes down to timing and planning.

- **Restaurant Week:** Restaurant associations around the country usually participate in Restaurant Week. Once or twice a year, restaurants will offer a special price for patrons. On average, lunch is usually between $20 and $25 and dinner runs between $20 and $50, and some are as little as $10. You can find the cities in your area by doing a simple search for Restaurant Week. Be sure to mark your calendars for dates in your area and make your reservations early. Once when I was in New York, I had the most amazing lobster dinner for a fraction of the usual cost. This is one of the best hidden secrets to dining on a dime.

- **Local culinary schools**: Years ago, I did a story on the fine dining experience offered at our local culinary school. It was an amazing deal. They offered an all-you-can-eat lunch and dinner buffet that was as delicious as any 5-star hotel. It was about $17 for the buffet or $25 for a three-course meal. So, check out any and all culinary schools in your area.

- **Rewards and loyalty programs:** Check out the websites at your favorite places to dine. Most larger restaurants and chains offer a perk if you sign up for their newsletter or loyalty card. Places like Panera Bread, Olive Garden, and Outback Steak House all have popular programs offering discounts, free birthday meals, drinks, desserts and more. Local restaurants have perks like these, as well, so check out the websites. One of our favorite local Italian restaurants offers a fixed-price menu which allows for four courses at a fraction of the a la carte cost.

- **Credit card perks:** Check your credit card and airline reward programs. If you earn points, you can often use them at restaurants for special discounts. Some credit cards cater to diners with extra points and discounts. You can find these partnerships on your credit card's website.

- **Membership discounts:** AAA and AARP are just two membership programs that offer restaurant discounts. If you are a member of a union or a credit union, check to see if they offer restaurant discounts as well.

- **Newspaper mailers and circulars:** Snail mail lives! You can find deals on meals in your mailbox.

- **Love at a late lunch:** Most restaurants serve the same or similar food at lunch as they do at dinner at a big savings. Choose to eat earlier and save 20% to 50%.

- **Deli delights:** Deli food has come a long way. You can find delicious, restaurant-quality food for less at certain delis or your grocery store's hot bar. During the summer, we go to our favorite spot in Healdsburg, we pick up gourmet salads and crab cakes and walk across the street to the park. We sit in the sun and listen to a local guitarist who plays in the park every weekend. For the evening, you can take it home, set the table, and light the candles.

- **Coupon and deal sites:** Groupon.com is a great place to find a great price on a great meal. Just plug in your zip code and you'll see hundreds of restaurants near you that are offering impressive discounts on a wide range of meals, from fast food to fancy. You can also register to get cash back when you dine at specific restaurants on Groupon's cashback program. As always read the fine print for restrictions.

- **High-end happy hours:** Some fine restaurants offer a special menu during earlier evening hours, usually 5 to 7 p.m. You can get drinks, cocktails, and special dishes for between 30% to 50% less. Don't forget to check out happy hours at local bars, hotels, and marinas, too!

- **Cook an exotic meal:** Check out your local ethnic grocery store for ingredients to create ethnic meals. Find the recipes online. Check out classic French, Italian, or German fine food offerings. Coq au Vin sounds fancy here in the U.S., but it doesn't cost much to put together this classic French chicken stew. Throw on some traditional music to that particular country. For this one you don't even need to leave the comfort of your own home to escape to an international destination.

- **Cooking classes:** This is a way to get an extra bang for your buck. I have taken small-group cooking classes and the best part is you get to eat what you cooked. So, it's a triple win: you are doing something fun with your partner, you are learning something new, and you get to enjoy a delicious meal. I paid $30 once for a lesson and we cooked up a yummy four course meal with wine.

Movies, Museums, and Sporting Events

- **Oscar movies:** Many movie theaters will offer a great deal right before the Academy Awards. You pay one price, usually about $35, but you are able to see all of the Best Picture nominations, regardless of how many movies are nominated.

- **The big screen:** Some movie theaters offer a monthly subscription pass, allowing you unlimited movies for a monthly fee. Packages range from about $18 to $24 a month. A general policy about movie discounts; matinees are usually less expensive. And buying your tickets at the box office instead of online will save you the convenience fees.

- **Museums:** Most museums have at least one day a month that's free to the public. Free is good, just keep in mind that there might be a lot of kids since schools take advantage of this free day. One of the best deals I have ever reported on, as well as taken advantage of myself, is buying a museum membership. Here's the deal: One annual individual or family membership may cost you between $65 and $150 dollars depending on the city and museum. But that membership will not only give you free admission, it will also allow free or low-cost admission to hundreds of other museums. Many large museums and science and technology centers are part of the North American Association of Reciprocal Museums, narmassociation.org. This group of distinguished museums reciprocate their membership with other museums. It's a great value for your entertainment buck. You also may be entitled to discounts on meals, parking, and the gift shop. Museums have some of the best event calendars with a range of attractions and activities. For example, here in San Francisco there is a weekly "date night" at the California Academy of Sciences. You and your date get admission to the natural history museum to enjoy live music, explore the coral reef, and visit the planetarium. It costs $30 a couple. Not free, but a great alternative to dinner or a movie.

- **Price clubs**: If you have a Costco membership, you can save on movie tickets and sporting events with their gift cards. The offers vary. Recently they had 10-packs available for AMC and Regal theaters. The savings came to a little more than $3 per ticket. The four-packs for Cinemark saved about $1.50 a ticket. Costco also sells discounted tickets to sporting events. Last summer friends of mine enjoyed field-level seats (which can run $60 to $100) at an Oakland A's game for less than $20 a ticket. What a luxury! Offers vary and are available in stores and online. Even if they are sold out online be sure to check your local store. If you are not a price club shopper, check your local grocery store and gas station for discounted gift cards. And save even more by using a cash-back credit card to buy them.

- **Minor league clubs:** Half the fun of going to a baseball game is going to the ballpark, rooting for a team, and of course the food. The thing is for major league games the tickets can cost you. Then you need to add in the parking or transportation, food and drinks. Opt for your team's minor league. You can have the same experience of going to a ballgame but for a fraction of the cost.

- **Theater, symphony, and opera:** Some local theater companies have free or low-cost tickets to their dress rehearsals. This way the cast gets comfortable in front of an audience and you get the deal. Some symphony and opera houses also sell tickets to dress rehearsals, as well as low-cost tickets to the standing sections. And don't forget your high school, college, and community theaters.

- **Apps, loyalty and rewards programs:** Some of the best deals around can be found by signing up for a newsletter, loyalty program, or app with your favorite theaters and teams. At the movies, you can find discounts and freebies on tickets, food, and drinks. For sports, there are often pre-season and in-season discounts on tickets. Friends of mine bought A's tickets online once and now routinely receive great ticket offers. For example, they bought a package for $30 that included two tickets, two hot dogs, and two beers. There was even discounted parking for $10.

Free or Almost Free: Possibilities Are Endless

When it comes to living a wonderful life, one of your most valuable assets is your imagination. (This is true no matter how much money you have in the bank!) Not every date needs to include a restaurant and the theater, some don't even need a price tag. Here are some ideas I love.

The Great Outdoors

- **Take a hike:** Find someplace new in your area and go exploring. In California, we have hundreds of miles of incredible regional and state parks to explore. I admire a friend of mine who one day after lunch spent hours hiking through majestic redwoods at a local park that she had never visited before, even though she has lived here for decades. Except for the gas, this outing was free, and it could pay off psychologically. If you haven't heard about *forest bathing,* it's the name coined in the '80s by the Japanese to describe the process of soaking up the sights, smells, and sounds of a natural setting to promote physiological and psychological health. Research at major universities all over the world shows that walking in the woods leads to feeling more relaxed and less stressed and even helps with depression, mood disorders, and other maladies. If you're not into nature, choose a nearby neighborhood or town you've never explored and spend an afternoon there. You can even keep a map of the places you've been.

- **Take a bike:** When I was a little girl, my favorite thing to do was hop on my blue bike. I even named her "Kitty Blue." To this day I love going for a bike ride and it is fun to do with a partner. Look for new local bike paths to explore. I have found local bike shops have maps to trails you might not know about. If you don't own a bike, you can rent a bike and helmet. Pack a lunch and pedal away.

- **Take up a sport:** It can be as simple as hitting your local park and taking advantage of their free tracks and circuit training routes. Or you can decide to start learning a new sport together like tennis. If you need to buy some equipment, check out a sporting resale shop like Play it Again Sports. These are places that sell used equipment at a fraction of the market price. Take some time to work on a fun fitness goal together.

- **Take a class:** I am always amazed at the variety of interesting classes available through local parks and recreation agencies. Adult schools and community centers also have a range of low-cost classes, including cooking, painting, dancing, yoga, and outdoor activities. These recurring classes mean you can have date night taken care of for weeks at a time. Plus, you could make new friends in your community while you're at it.

- **Take the plunge:** Some hotels and resorts will allow non-guests a day of pool access for a small fee. It's a great way to enjoy the ambiance of a luxury hotel without the price tag. You can also go for a swim at the public pool, a community public pool, or even your local city or college pool. You can also buy a day pass at a high-end health club and enjoy a day by their pool. If you are thinking of joining, most clubs will give you a free guest pass.

Free Fun: Foolproof Resources

There's a lot of information out there and it can be hard to avoid informational overload. There are so many fantastic resources for help finding free or almost-free events in our communities that I wanted to share how we dig up unique ways to spend time together.

- **Your local library**: A treasure trove of information on free or nearly free events in your community and often in a whole network of communities. Find yoga, art, language, readings, even low-cost farmers' markets inside the four walls of your local library. Check out the online calendar for ideas.

- **Community newspapers, event listings, and calendars:** Your city or town government website will often list events happening in your city. Where I live, we have musical concerts every Friday night during the summer. They are free, fun, and fabulous!

- **University or college calendars**: Music, literary readings, talks, and panel discussions are often free or low cost and open to the public. Check out their websites and sign up for activity alerts or newsletters to keep you up to date.

- **Your local parks:** Friends of mine recently took a free birdwatching hike to see some rare (for our area) bald eagles nesting near a local reservoir. There were about 20 people of all ages attending that day. The rangers had high quality bird viewing gear for all to get a glimpse. This was just one listing from a calendar that has literally hundreds of free events a month. Check out your local park's website.

- **Author events:** Check out your local book stores for visits by prominent authors.

- **Eventbrite:** Self-described as a global platform for live experiences that allows anyone to create, share, find, and attend events that fuel their passions and enrich their lives. Sounds good! A search of their events turned up gems like free kayaking in New York City, an archery range in Golden

Gate Park, and free game nights at various coin-operated game rooms. You can do a simple search on their site for a variety of free events in your area.

- **Goldstar:** Sign up for Goldstar in your area to get deals on everything from theatrical performances and comedy shows to outdoor events and lectures. I have even found deals on *Hamilton* tickets.

Helping Others

Volunteer with your partner. It's a way to help others while developing a closeness for a cause close to your hearts. You can deliver food to shut-ins, help at the Special Olympics, or spend time walking shelter dogs together. Sites like volunteermatch.org can help you find a perfect place to spend some time together while helping others.

6. FAMILY FUN

When I was growing up, we didn't schedule play dates. We threw open the front door and ran outside to see who could come out to play. As soon as school let out on Fridays, I would meet three of my closest friends; Adrienne, Ginny, and Jill. We would meet at Adrienne's house because they had an in-law apartment. The four of us would turn this three-room playhouse into our "City." We would each have our own "house" and using our dolls, created our families. We wrote out blank checks so we could spend money for things we needed. We would be storeowners, bankers, and teachers. From Friday until late

Sunday afternoon we would play in our city. There is a lot to be said for giving kids an empty room and letting their imaginations flow.

Today, parents are much more involved in encouraging kids to use their imaginations. We have access to the Internet which lets us find worlds of opportunity in our own back yard. When my son was little, I tried to keep him entertained with activities that met two criteria: fun and free! As I began reporting on family-fun-for-free stories, I received an overwhelming response from viewers. Everyone was searching for ways to create affordable but rich lasting memories.

While every family is different, virtually every child on the planet thrives with personal attention from caring people. When it comes to saving money on fun family activities, the resources seem limitless. It is possible to keep the kids entertained without breaking the bank. From free bowling to a museum membership that gets you into hundreds of places, there are dozens of ways for families to have fun on a budget. As times change, some of these resources may make adjustments for social distancing or be temporarily on hold. But you'll have plenty of ideas on hand the next time your kids complain that they're bored.

Plan Ahead: Idea Central

Every parent knows that family life is easier with planning, especially once kids come along. We all have calendars to schedule school events. Why not create one for free-time ideas?

Just pencil in the possibilities and you'll soon have many days' worth of activities at your fingertips.

Getting Started: Tried and True Things to Do

- **Community calendars:** Many communities publish seasonal calendars that include free and low-cost classes and activities for everyone. Expand your field of vision by checking out calendars at your local college or university where you'll find free concerts, talks, and hands-on experiences for kids.

- **Science and discovery museums, aquariums, and more:** The San Francisco Bay Area, where I raised my son, literally has dozens of museums that kids enjoy. One of the biggest bangs for a parent's buck is to buy a family membership to a museum or science center that is part of the North American Association of Reciprocal Museums. Most memberships include a free admission for a family of four and will cost you around $100 for a year. You can pay a bit more for additional family members. Not only will you have access to this museum, but also free or low-cost access to hundreds of other museums, discovery centers, and more. We never ran out of things to do. Check calendars for special hands-on activities and classes. One other perk: for some facilities that have outside picnic areas, you can reserve these and have your kids' birthday party there.

- **Movie passes:** Theaters often offer kids' movie days during summer mornings for very affordable prices.

- **Library systems:** Make sure you check your library system's website. While many of us are familiar with our local library, you would be surprised at what's available in nearby cities and towns. A family friend recently attended a free art class offered by a local illustrator at a library one town over. Had she not gone online to check she wouldn't have known about it. And libraries are not just for reading anymore. Many offer classes, talks, and even deals on museum tickets and events.

- **Local, state, and national parks:** Look for yearly passes that quickly pay for themselves with more than one family visit. Sign up for alerts so you're up-to-date on special activities offered throughout the year. Even if you don't sign up for membership, local and regional parks often offer free activities. One Bay Area regional park near me even has digital learning activities for kids like nature journaling, building a bird feeder, and creating scavenger hunts.

- **Wildlife organizations and environmental groups:** Groups like the Audubon Society and the Sierra Club offer local calendar events designed to create life-long nature lovers from a young age.

- **Home-schooling websites:** Resources abound for parents who home school their children. A simple Google search of "home school activities" provides hundreds of ideas for free and low-cost activities for kids at every grade level.

- **Online learning:** While we like limiting screen time, there are some incredible free resources online for kids who have special interests. If your child likes birds, the outstanding Cornell Lab of Ornithology has special fun learning sections for students of all grade levels, starting with kindergarten. You can find other educational resources from PBS, the BBC, and National Geographic, to name a few.

- **Free food:** Some chain restaurants like Denny's, Ruby Tuesday, and Marie Callender's offer free kid's meals on certain days of the week with the purchase of an adult meal.

- **History walk:** Do a self-guided tour of your town highlighting local historical sites along the way. Bring along a sketch pad and colored pencils and have the kids draw pictures of what life was like back in the day.

- **Special camps:** There are a variety of free summer camps for kids with special needs. If your child has a chronic disease or disability, there may be a free camp in your area or close by. My friend's daughter has Crohn's disease. Every summer from the time she was in third grade until she graduated from high school, she attended a camp with other kids who have Crohn's disease. It was free and fun. She still talks about these wonderful summer memories — even though she's 28 years old now. The benefits linger long after summer is over; my friend's daughter is still in touch with some of her former fellow campers.

Helping Others

Volunteering together is not only fun and free but it is so rewarding. And it teaches our children at a young age the importance of giving back and the greater good. The options are endless for volunteering. Whether it's an annual event like Coastal Cleanup or a weekly visit to the SPCA to walk dogs, you'll create lasting memories by volunteering with your kids. Habitat for Humanity, Meals on Wheels, The Literacy Project, and the YMCA are just a few of the nationally known organizations that accept young volunteers.

7. FINANCING COLLEGE 101

One of the most common questions I have been asked over the years comes from parents. It would go something like: "How can I afford to cover my monthly expenses and pay for my children's college education?" Or, "Should I save for a house, retirement, or college for my children?"

There is a weight on our shoulders of wanting to provide the best for our kids even when our means are limited. But you can lift that weight and be proactive. Fortunately, it's never too early to start. While at CBS, I interviewed Gen and Kelly Tanabe, the authors of *1001 Ways to Pay for College* and many other books on paying for higher education. It was one of the most eye-opening interviews I have ever done. They talked about all of the unique scholarships out there and how funds actually can go unused. What!?! Money that is left on the table? There are so many opportunities to help families navigate the financial costs for their child's education, it's just a matter of knowing when and where to look.

We all pay higher prices now than we did 20 years ago for almost everything, but the consistently increasing rate of college costs is staggering. The "Trends in College Pricing Report" shows 2018 students paid 213% more for a state school than students in 1998. Private schools cost 129% more. While almost no one pays the full sticker price for a college, *U.S. News & World Report* says that the average student in 2020 graduates $29,000 in debt. Multiply this by more than one student and you can see why most parents lose a lot of sleep trying to strategize a plan for college. The good news is there are a variety of ways to shave costs even if you haven't started saving yet. Class is in session so let's get started.

College Savings Success Basics

The thought of coming up with hundreds of thousands of dollars for a big-ticket item like college that's years off in the future while struggling to make ends meet at the moment can result in saving paralysis. Many of us simply can't bear to look at the overwhelming details of what seems like an impossible task. But this is a mistake. Taking action, no matter where you are in the process of saving, will help and make a difference.

When it comes to saving for college, you can start before your baby is even born. And don't think that having too much in savings will hurt your chances of receiving financial aid in the future. Experts say this is a big misconception; the extremely complicated formulas for financial aid take income into account much more than savings. Retirement accounts are not considered in the formula. Unless it's an emergency, withdrawing from your retirement account is not a good idea.

Here are some ways families have helped their kids through school while taking on little or no debt.

Before Baby's Born

When you're planning gender reveal parties and baby showers, think of tuition and books along with the bottles and binkies.

• Set up your own 529 college savings plan and add it to the registry. These state government and institution sponsored programs allow anyone to make contributions easily, and they can have significant tax benefits. Grandparents who want to help can also easily set up these accounts and many funds are set up with grandparents' tax needs in mind. It pays to shop around, because the features and fees vary. If you start early enough and make regular contributions, these plans can really lighten the college cost load that many families will find themselves shouldering. 529 Plans are not all created equal, though. Morningstar rates these plans regularly.

- Start a savings account at your bank. While this probably won't yield the kind of income and tax advantages you'll get with a 529 plan, it's a start. Check with your bank to see whether the plan should be in your name or your child's, because this can affect financial aid in the long run. You can also talk to your bank about different savings tools that may pay higher interest than a regular passbook account.

- Spend to save. Consider using credit cards like Upromise where your points or awards go into a 529 account.

High School

If you haven't started saving by high school, the odds of saving $100,000 or more in four years is highly unlikely. Here are some free or low-cost strategies that can help significantly.

- **Advanced placement classes:** Serious students can take advanced placement classes that will satisfy some college-level requirements at some schools. This can shorten the length of time it takes to get a degree. If you can graduate in three years instead of four, you've saved yourself thousands of dollars in tuition, plus room and board. Just make sure to check if the institution you want to attend accepts the classes. Some do, some don't.

- **Start college early:** Here in California, some high school juniors and seniors are allowed to start taking college classes at community colleges, where the tuition is negligible. These classes can count toward college graduation, and can shorten the time it takes to get a degree at a four-year school.

Applying for College

When the junior year of high school kicks in the financial reality can come into terrifying focus. Now families need to consider which schools *and* payment plans will work best for their finances.

Choosing a School

Every family's different. Whether your child is heading for the Ivy League, a state school, or a certificate program, there are dozens of proven ways to manage the costs, even if you have nothing saved. Choosing the right school will make a big difference in the final price tag.

- **Certificate programs**: Not every child needs a college degree to earn a good living. Many families save themselves money and heartache by skipping the college degree and heading to certificate programs in technology, healthcare, and the trades. Plumbers, dental assistants, court reporters, and x-ray technicians are just a few of the high-paying positions people can score through certificate training programs.

- **Online college programs:** Compare the costs between attending college online and on campus. More and more colleges are offering this as an option. Additionally, you will save money on commuting or room and board.

- **Community college:** The U.S. Department of Education reports the average price for two years of community college is less than half the cost of a single year at a four-year state school. Your student can save by taking as many elective courses as possible towards their major at a community college. As an added bonus, some community colleges are feeder programs for state university schools. For example, while very few people qualify for the University of California at Berkeley right out of high school, the UC system saves a number of third-year spots for community college transfers.

- **State schools:** The average cost of tuition and fees in 2018-2019 for a private college was $35,676 – significantly higher than the average tuition and fees at public universities and colleges, which is $9,716 for in-state students according to the U.S. Annual Survey of Colleges.

- **State universities:** In general, most state universities are more expensive than state colleges, but if your student's heart is set on a state university there are strategies for saving there, as well.

- **Private colleges and universities:** These schools have the highest price tag right out of the gate, but don't assume you could never afford a top-tier private school. A well-endowed top tier school could wind up costing you less than a cash-strapped state university if your student qualifies for admission.

Financial Aid

Taking the time to figure out how much financial aid your family is eligible for is crucial. Don't assume you won't benefit from doing some legwork here, even if you earn a good income and have assets available. Typically, no one pays full freight at the most expensive colleges, so the time and effort could pay off. There may also be tax credits you can qualify for. For example, check to see if the student would qualify for the American Opportunity Credit. This can potentially give up to a $2,500 tax credit.

About FAFSA: Free Application for Student Aid

The Free Application for Student Aid (FAFSA) is a standard federal application that all students fill out for financial aid. Triple-check your FAFSA forms. Simple errors can have a major impact. The rules can change every year, so don't assume that you know how to fill out the form because you've done it before. Many high schools provide guidance for filling out FAFSA. For more on help with FAFSA see the resources at the end of this chapter. Seek out the help of school counselors who are familiar with these forms and the process.

Grants and Scholarships: Free Money

While there may be no such thing as a free lunch, there is free money for college. Grants and scholarships don't have to be paid back. There is a wide array of possibilities. I will warm you up with some basic background then point you towards some incredible resources that will make your search easier.

- **Grants:** While many people think of grants and scholarships as the same thing, there is a slight difference. Grants are based on need; scholarships are based on merit. Grants are usually awarded based on your or your family's financial situation.

- **Federal grants:** Federal Supplemental Educational Opportunity Grants (FSEOG), Iraq and Afghanistan Service Grants, Teacher Education Assistance for College and Higher Education (TEACH) Grants. Resources for more information on federal grants can be found at the end of this chapter.

- **State grants:** States often help make up for shortfalls provided by federal grants. For instance, Minnesota Office of Higher Education provides state grants to low- and moderate-income students, with nearly 80% of funds distributed to students with family incomes below a certain amount per year. Check out what's available in your state.

- **Diversity grants:** There are a variety of need-based grants available for groups that have been historically disadvantaged. If you're low-income and are a woman, a veteran, African American, Hispanic, Native American, disabled, or a member of other groups, you may find grants available in your state. In Alaska for example, The Bureau of Indian Education Higher Education Grant Program (BIA) supplements other grants for Native Americans and Native Alaskans. See more resources at the end of the chapter.

- **Scholarships:** Scholarships are based on merit, but you don't have to be a scholar to qualify for scholarship dollars. Here are just a few of the organizations that routinely hand out merit-based money.

- federal, state, and local government agencies

- colleges and universities

- corporations

- professional organizations

- charitable foundations

- advocacy groups

And to prove that not all scholarships go to the person with the highest GPA, here is a list of the reasons you can find yourself earning a scholarship.

- **Average academic performance scholarships:** You can't be a total slouch, but these scholarships consider the person as a whole. The judges could consider character, community service, and other qualities along with an average GPA.

- **Athletic scholarships**

- **Scholarships for minorities**

- **Scholarships for women**

- **Creative scholarships:** Art scholarships, music scholarships, and even dance scholarships usually involve an audition of some sort, and can help you get through art school or an art program at a university.

- **Community service scholarships and unusual scholarships:** There's money out there for students with unique interests or qualifications. For example, if you want to major in telecommunications at Ball State there is the David Letterman Scholarship. Or say you can answer questions about fire sprinklers. You may qualify for the American Fire Sprinkler Scholarship. Even having the right last name can help. Harvard University has special funds available if your last name is Hudson, Thayer, or Bright, to name a few. Are you left-handed? Red-headed? Tall? Check resources at the end of the chapter for ways to find out if your unique quality qualifies for college cash.

- **Health-related scholarships:** For students who have specific medical conditions, certain foundations offer scholarships. For example, there are funds for up to $15,000 from AbbVie Immunology Scholarship for students with disabilities and chronic diseases. Also, there is a range of scholarships for student cancer survivors and oncology patients. These are just two examples. If your child has a medical condition, please check with the foundation or organization for that particular condition for specific scholarship resources.

In College: What Next?

Once your student is in college, expenses do continue. Keep up to date on scholarship, grant, and loan deadlines. There may be opportunities for your child to work on-campus earning money or credit toward their tuition. Graduate work programs are available and kids should look into graduate work programs for possible employment in their area of interest.

Fellowships allow for students to continue their education and work experience. The costs are covered and in return, at one point after completion, the student will do some work as a condition of the award.

Helping Others

A friend of mine volunteered with an organization that helped with the preparation and paperwork for college bound students. Often times these organizations serve the inner cities or lower-income communities. The specific goal is to make sure every financial assistance opportunity open to them is explored. It is very rewarding volunteer work and exciting when the kids you work with are able to attend college. You can search your local communities for programs near you.

8. BE HEALTHY, BE WELL, BE SAVVY

"Nature intended that everybody should be happy. We have failed to learn the true lesson of life if we have not every day surmounted a fear. The habit of idle discontent is based upon ridiculous hopes and wishes. Circumstances alone cannot bring happiness. Life is richer in joy than in sorrow. Happiness comes from a contented spirit, a pure heart and a kind and loving disposition. It comes from humility and charity, with a generous appreciation of others, and a modest opinion of self."

I found these words in one of my dad's notebooks. It seems as though my parents and their friends lived by them to the letter.

The "Gang", as they called themselves, met after the war. As people were starting to put their lives back together, a neighborhood priest thought he should start a type of social club. The goal was to get these youngsters back to enjoying what was left of their youth. There would be dances and roller-skating, picnics and movies. And it was here that 6 guys met 6 gals. They fell in love, got married, stayed married and 75 years later they are still the best of friends. When I was at CBS 5, we did a primetime special on this unique love story for which we were honored to win an Emmy. The gang was there that evening. When they announced the winner, I watched the Gang jump from their seats in excitement while the room gave them a standing ovation. It was one of the best nights of my life, the kind you don't want to end. I was fortunate to grow up with the Gang. Each of them is fearless. Which makes me reflect on the sentence from my dad's quote, "We have failed to learn the true lesson of life if we have not every day surmounted a fear." There have been many times in my life when my fears have gotten in the way of my moving forward and affected my sense of well-being. These words helped keep me on track when I wanted to run away from scary situations, or was too paralyzed to do anything. I think most of us can relate to this feeling at one time or another and know that life viewed through fear-colored glasses is not our best life.

When financial challenges cause fear, it is tough to access a feeling of well-being. Fear, even terror, sets in. But the fact is, when going through financial pressures, it's more important than ever to be able to decompress and feel a sense of serenity inside.

With some inner peace I find the strength to respond to situations thoughtfully, rather than react in the spur of the moment to minimize my fear.

When I think of *The Joy of $aving*, I never think of deprivation or hardship. I think about using the resources I have to live my best life. Most of my best life has very little to do with dollars. Of course, we all need to know we can support our basic needs, but once those are met, I believe that the best things in life are truly free, or almost free. My peace of mind and feelings of wellbeing are two of my most prized possessions. And when I am able to live in that state, I am content and happy. For me, that means creating a warm and friendly home where I can be with my family and friends in a beautiful, safe environment. My vacations don't need to be lavish; a new locale close to home can be just as exciting a find as a Paris café. I value my wellness and personal care and I have a spending plan for them. This spending category includes meditation, exercise, and personal care products. Basically, everything that doesn't fall into the medical category but is important for my sense of wellbeing goes into the personal care category. The best part is it doesn't cost much money to create a wellness program.

The other line, "It's about being the best you can be," makes me wonder: How do we become the best we can be? And when do we know we have reached our best? My feeling is it is a process, part of life's journey. For me, living in a state of gratitude and contentment with the aspiration to learn and grow feels like the healthiest place to be. While I haven't met anyone who lives a life totally free of fear, my dad's "healthy" outlook has helped me learn to face life's challenges without being totally blind-sided by fear.

So, what does it mean to be well? I look at it from the inside out. As my dad wrote, "a healthy spirit and a positive outlook." I know during the times I was struggling financially, it was tough to have that positive outlook. I was stuck in feelings of shame and blame. But I was able to shake myself out of the doldrums. Fortunately, I realized that my negative thoughts were actually more detrimental than my financial situation. I was a young, single mom not making much money and I needed to make a shift. I started focusing on what I could create rather than what I didn't have at the moment. But when I started telling myself a different story, everything changed. I flipped the statement, "You are in debt and will never get out of it" to "You can earn extra money, get out of debt, and start to save." What we tell ourselves is powerful and the first step in creating our sense of wellbeing.

Mindfulness and Spirituality

There was a time in my life when everything hit me at once. My son's dad died within five months of a cancer diagnosis. Six weeks later my beloved brother-in-law died. My 13-year old son and I were struggling to make it through each day. Wellbeing was not in my vocabulary. I was in emotional turmoil, and every day was a challenge. During this time, I was working as an on-camera reporter and had to put on a happy face from 9 a.m. to 5:30 p.m. when I would sign off air for the day. It was tough to do, but I would put my feelings in a box that I would shelve until I got home. I also gained about 20 pounds, as I seemed to eat my way through this stressful time.

Then one Sunday morning I didn't have the interest or energy to get out of bed. As I lay there, I recalled a conversation I had with a woman several months earlier. She told me about a spiritual service she attended on Sundays at a place called Unity. She said it helped her make sense out of life and was her place for finding inner peace. I thought I could use something like that, and called to find out where my local Unity Church was. I decided to go that day and it was a game-changer for me.

I couldn't control much of what was happening in my life, but I finally realized I *could* control my response to it. I realized I was not alone with life's struggles. Finding a community that you can turn to for inspiration, insight, and support costs absolutely nothing and is one of the most valuable things you can do for your state of wellbeing. It doesn't have to be religious, it just needs to be a community that helps you feel accepted and supported.

I continued my connection with Unity even as my life got back on track. It became my weekly reboot. In 2014 I felt I needed more focus in my life. I am a multi-tasker and tend to be distracted - I have a "monkey-mind" as the Buddhists call it. Friends had suggested meditation, but like many people, I felt there would be no way I could learn to meditate. Fortunately, I was wrong about that. I took a course to learn Transcendental Meditation, or TM. As I began to incorporate this practice into my daily life, I could literally feel a new sense of calm, inner wellbeing that I'd never had access to before. It has been one of the best things I have ever done for myself.

When I was growing up, meditation was considered a counter culture practice for rock stars and hippies, certainly not an essential element of overall healthcare. But times have changed. Today, mindfulness meditation is prescribed by physicians for a host of ailments to treat pain, anxiety, and burnout. There's encouraging research being done on its effect on PTSD, depression, and chronic pain, for children as well as adults. There are many different types of meditation practice. For me, TM worked. You can find meditation centers, virtual meditations, podcasts, and apps to help you learn about and connect with a meditation practices that feels right for you.

A study by the Centers for Disease Control and Prevention (CDC) looked at changes in attitude towards complementary practices like yoga, meditation, and chiropractic care in the U.S. over a five-year period. Of the three, yoga was the most popular, but the fastest growing was meditation, which had tripled in popularity between 2012 and 2017. Those numbers continue to rise as healthcare experts, insurance companies, and workplaces seek to promote practices that enhance wellbeing. Research into benefits continues around the world. Right now, here are several things we know about how meditation can help you maintain health and wellbeing.

- **Stress reduction:** Research suggests that mindfulness breathing can quiet the fight-or-flight response in our body, calming the area of the brain that can cause a cascade of stress responses.

- **Focus:** Regular meditation helps us concentrate. Even a short 10 minutes a day can result in benefits.

- **Self-compassion:** If you are the type of person who has a harsh inner critic or is constantly beating yourself up, mindfulness practices focused on loving-kindness can boost your compassion for yourself and others.

- **Mental health:** Mindfulness can lead to overall improvements in mental health.

Check with your insurance plan and see if they offer a class or other benefits relating to meditation.

Use It or Lose It

The part of high school science that we should all keep in mind is Isaac Newton's First Law of Motion: A body at rest remains at rest. This is one scientific fact that I know is true. My body wants to remain at rest, and the longer it stays at rest, the more it wants to stay there. The motivation, time, and dedication it takes to get the exercise we need can be elusive. Sometimes we might believe that spending money on exercise will magically transform us into the svelte pictures of fitness we see in the ads.

A report from the Global Wellness Institute, a nonprofit organization focused on preventative health and wellness, found that Americans spent $264.6 billion on physical activity in 2018, far more than all other countries. The U.S. leads the world in spending for every category: fitness classes ($37 billion); sports and recreation ($58 billion); apparel and footwear ($117 billion); equipment and supplies ($37.5 billion); mindful movement, such as yoga ($10 billion); and related technology ($8.1 billion). Yet studies have shown that America is one of the least healthy countries on the planet, with skyrocketing rates of obesity and diabetes.

We don't need a lot of fancy clothes, equipment, or gym memberships to stay in good shape. You just need to move your body and that can be absolutely free. Find something you really enjoy, like dancing, gardening, or bike riding and have an intention to get active at least 5 to 6 days a week. One of my favorite fitness gurus, Jaime McFaden, has a great way of reminding me how important this kind of self-care is. "Your health account is like a bank account - what you put in you can get out. Fitness doesn't cost much. In fact, walking, jogging, swimming, and bodyweight exercises can be done with zero cost. The cost of diet pills, liposuction, medical bills will add up quickly so take care of your health NOW. Love yourself enough to take care of your body + mind. Moving just 20-30 minutes per day can keep you healthy and away from chronic diseases." It's much easier to stick to an intention when you love the activity you choose.

I will admit I am not a huge fan of exercising. I do find if I decide to ride my bike for 15 minutes it will often turn into 30. When I put music on and just dance around, I do break a sweat. If you are short on time you can search online for quick workouts. You don't need to buy much of anything to move your body. Housecleaning, walking, dancing, gardening, climbing stairs, hiking, biking, and swimming are all excellent ways to get your muscles moving and your heart rate up — and you probably already own everything you need to get started now. In fact, just walking my little dog, Puccini, helps me log about 10,000 steps a day. Remember to check with your doctor before you start an exercise routine regardless of whether you have health concerns or not.

Skip the Gym Membership: Exercise at Home

Every January when I was a consumer reporter, we did the same news story about gym memberships. You know the story. The first week in January gyms around the country are jammed with people resolving to get healthy in the new year. By February, their numbers have thinned back almost to pre-New Year levels. Some people never show up again after the first time.

Unless you know that you'll actually use a gym membership, make sure that you are able to cancel it without huge penalties. If you know yourself well enough to know you won't be showing up often, there are some great alternatives that will help you stay in shape while saving at the same time.

- **Fitness equipment:** It's really easy to find pre-owned gear at used sporting goods stores, yard sales, and online. You can also check sites like Freecycle and the free sections of sites like Craigslist. Similar to cars, new treadmills and weight machines lose a lot of their value when they leave the store; you can potentially save hundreds of dollars shopping for used models.

- **Exercise online:** There are literally thousands of workout routines on YouTube for every age, exercise level, and kind of exercise. Find a teacher or a routine you like and try to set consistent times to exercise every day, or as often as you can. You can find very famous and very expensive teachers who offer their workout routines for free this way.

- **Join a sports club:** Do you love basketball, soccer, or other team sports? Look for a local league and sign up. Some sports have fees for use of the fields and administrative costs. The costs are usually nominal, the camaraderie: priceless.

- **Use public facilities:** Many communities have free tennis courts, low cost public pools, and community exercise classes. This can be a great way to get in shape and connect with your neighbors at the same time. Sometimes public pools are in beautiful areas and you'll feel like you are at a resort while visiting.

- **Join a Zoom class:** While many are not free, Zoom video classes are more personalized online classes where you can get advice and feedback from the instructor, who can watch your technique as you exercise. These classes are especially helpful for martial arts, Pilates, and yoga, but they can also be great for weight training and for anyone who needs some outside support for motivation.

- **Teach a class:** If you love your exercise program, see if you can get certified as a teacher. Not only will you be spending time doing something you love but you can earn money while doing it.

- **Recreation centers:** Some of the best classes at the best prices are through your local rec center. They run the gamut: yoga, dance, tap, Pilates, and more. Typically, you pay one rate for several weeks of classes.

Budget Beauty: Personal Care Products

It's hard to put an exact number on how much Americans spend on personal care products annually, but it is safe to say it's well over $100 billion. Sales of products including shampoo, conditioner, shaving cream, cleansers, lotions, facial moisturizers, and cosmetics are big business. And the relationship between price and quality of personal care products is tricky. Is there a big difference between what's inside the $50 bottle of conditioner and what's in the $5 bottle? Yes and no. It depends what's actually *in* the bottle, so label reading is a must. Here's what to look for when trying to decide how to spend your personal care dollars.

Read the Labels

These are some items that you should feel good about seeing on an ingredient list. You might see these in a wide variety of personal care products, including shampoo, conditioner, shaving cream, cleansers, lotions, and facial moisturizers.

- Oils from nuts and seeds

- Avocado and avocado oils

- Oatmeal

- Cocoa butter and shea butter

- Fruit, nut, seed, and plant extracts

It's also common to see the following ingredients, which are usually safe to use.

- Glycerin

- Sodium citrate and citric acid

- Vitamins, including vitamin E and Panthenol (which is a form of vitamin B)

If you know how to evaluate an ingredient list, you can try to find the same ingredients found in high-end products in more affordable versions. If two products contain very similar ingredient lists, in a similar order, but one costs three times as much, it's possible that the extra expense is due to marketing and packaging. Save your money and go with the cheaper option.

Some common ingredients in personal care products have been cause for concern over the years. Reading literature about these ingredients can help you decide whether you want to use them yourself.

- **Sulfates**. Common in shampoo, body wash, and other cleansers, sulfates help create lather. However, in the process, they can strip hair and skin of necessary oils and lead to drying. According to some experts, people with naturally curly, dry, or brittle hair should consider avoiding shampoos containing sulfates. The same goes for cleansers for people with sensitive skin. Fortunately, the recent consumer demands for sulfate-free shampoos and cleansers have encouraged more manufacturers to produce sulfate-free products.

- **Phthalates and parabens**. Phthalates and parabens are common in personal care products including shampoo, conditioner, body wash, shaving cream, and lotion. The EPA has extensive information about these chemicals on their website. While at CBS 5, I did an in-depth story on these chemicals. One recommendation from experts was for people who are particularly sensitive, including pregnant women and very young children, to consider avoiding products with phthalates and parabens to be on the safe side. Again, with increasing demand for products without these ingredients, there is a growing variety of choices available at stores.

- **Synthetic fragrances and dyes**. If your personal care product smells good or has a pleasant color, check the ingredient list to see where those nice colors and smells are coming from. If plant, fruit, or flower extracts are used, the fragrance or dye is less likely to be an irritant. You can also look for products that are labeled as "hypoallergenic," meaning they are less likely to contain ingredients that commonly cause allergic reactions. Keep in mind that the term "hypoallergenic" isn't regulated, so if you know that you have sensitivities to certain ingredients, you should still look at the label closely.

Remember, the term "natural" isn't regulated, so if you see "natural" on the label, check the ingredients to see if it is what you're looking for. The term "organic" however *is* regulated, so the product must contain at least 95% organically produced ingredients. It's a good idea to check the return policy for any product that you purchase should you have a reaction.

Compare Prices

Online searches make it extremely easy to compare prices. If you find a product that interests you, check the websites of the top big box retailers (such as Target and Walmart), drug stores (such as Walgreens and CVS), and online retailers (such as Amazon.com and Drugstore.com) to compare prices and availability. If a retailer doesn't publish a price online, don't be afraid to pick up the phone and call to ask them for a price check. Most drug stores offer rewards or loyalty programs for free. If you do nothing else, do this. Join their program and shop when items are on special. Additionally, these programs allow for some type of rewards or bucks to use towards future purchases. I did a story on this and by using the rewards, coupons, and the cash-back perk, I was able to cut my bill by 40%.

Doing your online research also affords the opportunity to read reviews from other consumers, and many sites list ingredients so you can do a virtual "back of the label" check before you make a purchase.

Makeup Online

Some of the best deals for makeup can be found from the comforts of your own home while shopping online. Since online shopping has become so popular, there are some makeup brands that are only available through the Internet. These brands tend to be priced like drugstore brands, and are known for their quality. When ordering products online make sure to factor in the cost of shipping, which can be more expensive than the product itself in some cases. Most stores will allow for returns if you get an allergic reaction to a product you purchase. For products I am trying for the first time, I save my receipt and also the packaging it came in just in case I need to return it.

Helping Others

If you're like me you have a box of those little soaps, lotions, and shampoos from your hotel stays. I used to stay at the W Hotel in NYC for a show that I would regularly work on. I loved that they had Bliss brand skincare products for their toiletries. I would come home with my little leftovers. Over the years, I had quite a collection. When the California fires were ravaging our state, a local business did a collection of these items. I put little gift bags together filled with the Bliss products. It felt so good to know that someone who could really use them was going to be able to enjoy the products. There are several programs that collect these little treasures. The Salvation Army and Operation: Care and Comfort both accept unused items. Do a search for a resource in your area.

If you are trained in the area of meditation, you can check with local churches and community programs to offer your services. This is a gift that will keep on giving.

And if you want to share a wonderful story about love and friendship, you can find the show I mentioned on the Gang. You can watch it on Vimeo.com. Just enter "Six Degrees of Love".

9. DECORATING ON A DIME

As my cameraman and I drove along the water to the outer part of San Francisco, the landscape suddenly changed; the iconic beauty becoming grittier and more industrial as we headed south. Suddenly we entered a large outdoor salvage area, a treasure trove of unique objects that had been stripped from homes being remodeled. Row after row of claw-foot bathtubs, chandeliers, ornate door knobs, and antique stoves were on display. As the saying goes, one man's junk is another man's treasure. The owner of this salvage yard was one of the first people I met benefiting from new laws that prohibited discarding housing fixtures from historic homes. I specifically remember these beautiful antique doorknobs that came from a house in a very affluent area. I think one of the best ways to not only save money but also the environment is to seek out these priceless treasure troves. There are a wide variety of salvage stores these days. Some take anything, others are focused on different times like the Victorian or Colonial eras. Search online for re-use or recycling centers to find stores like this near you.

When I was in my 20s, years before I reported on this story, I had already started converting junk to treasures. And my very small basement studio was a testament to what you can create with a little imagination and even less money. It was so cute and I made the most of every square foot. I decorated it on a dime and made it my own. I really loved it. Transforming a house into a home should be fun and exciting. And you can do this if you know the tricks of the trade.

What Designers Know

Before you take the department store by storm, look around the room you want to transform. Is it cluttered? Dark? Overcrowded with furniture, floor lamps, or other objects that don't serve you? Here is where you need to make a decision to get rid of as much clutter as you can. Clutter in this case is old artwork, tchotchkes, figurines, photos, books, piles of anything. Once you have created a room that's less cluttered, you'll notice you've already made a big improvement. After that, here are some tried-and-true methods designers use to get the most bang for the least buck.

- **Rearrange the furniture**: You can do research online to find cool floorplans and other ideas that you wouldn't think of without professional advice. Take into account the size of the room and how you can make the most of it. Apartment Therapy is a site loaded with ideas on how you can create more with less space.

- **Paint:** The quickest way to freshen up a room or give it a new feel is to paint it. And don't stop with the walls. You can use paint on furniture, ceilings, floors, and patios. You can paint accessories. The list is almost endless. Always seal unused paint tightly to store it. Make sure you label the cans so you remember which room you originally used it for when you need future touch-ups. You never know when it might come in handy. And if you just need a little for a special project, you can buy small tester cans. If you are renting your home, make sure you get permission from the landlord to paint. They might even offer to cover the cost of the materials.

- **Lighting:** Make sure your space glows. Let the natural light from outside in by getting rid of dark shades or drapes. Electricians can add dimmers to light switches or you can add floor and table lamps to rooms with overhead lights. A very cool way to add special lighting is with battery powered stick-on lights. You can add these to the underside of kitchen cabinets, book cases, and plants. Add strings of lights to your patio. I did this and it brought the entire backyard to life.

- **Art:** You can find impressive, room-altering artworks at thrift stores, yard sales, online, and at off-price stores like Ross and Marshalls. Buy from students. Your local school probably has more than one yearly art exhibition of talented young artists of all ages. You can blow up photos to wall size at your local office supply or print shop. Or search through DIY projects online to discover fun ways to create your own art from things like old window frames, pallets, or other found objects. If you are having an event or just want to enjoy a higher-priced piece of art, look into a local art rental shop. I once did a story on local artists at Fort Mason in San Francisco. A couple of times a year they would open up their studios for a public sale. You could find fabulous, original artwork at extremely reasonable prices. My favorite art in my home is created by a talented artist, Michelle Brantley. She has a rare gift of being able to create a painting from a photograph. I have sent her photos of special times or memories with family, and I receive back a painting that is identical to the photo. Additionally, her prices are beyond reasonable!

Some Bargains Don't Sit Right with Me

While it's easy to find low-priced furniture stores offering everything for rock-bottom prices, it's important to remember that you can find high quality used or gently used pieces for similar prices. Really cheap furniture usually doesn't have a long shelf life with regular wear and tear. When it comes to furniture and cars, sometimes the used version affords a much greater value than something brand new at a similar price. Check with your local home consignment stores for some of the best deals. Another way to save is to buy slipcovers for your sofa and chairs. I did this for years before I had saved enough money to purchase a new sofa at an outlet. These days the slipcovers are lovely and fit well. No matter where you buy your furniture, here is one tip you must use when buying larger pieces like a sofa: measure the doorways and the furniture before buying to make sure it will fit through the door. I have heard from viewers over the years with horror stories of not being able to fit the furniture through the door.

The Hunt Is On!

While most of us head to the big stores to find the furniture we need, you don't have to be a victim to the prices and designs that are currently in stock when you need something. Here are some ways to save a chunk of change while creating a unique look. Just make sure you take measurements before you buy anything, whether it's in a regular store or online.

- **Get inspired**: Check out social media sites and marketplaces like Pinterest, Instagram, and Etsy for creative bargain decorating ideas from design professionals and amateurs. You can also search bargain bloggers for ideas.

- **Consignment vs. thrift:** Consignment stores receive merchandise directly from the seller and share the profits from the sale. Thrift stores survive on donations. The prices at consignment stores can be higher than at thrift stores, but the quality usually is, too, as they have the final say over what is offered for sale in their stores. Thrift stores run on donations, so you are at the mercy of mounds of merchandise that people want to part with. You'll usually spend less time digging at consignment stores and the overall quality tends to be better. That said, you can find deals of a lifetime at thrift stores. I certainly have.

- **Re-use:** As mentioned above, consignment stores, yard sales, Habitat for Humanity Restore, thrift stores, Freecycle, Nextdoor, Craigslist are all prime locations for incredible finds on furniture and home improvement projects.

- **Hardware store:** The hardware store is home to some of the best money saving hacks around. Buy a can of paint to create a whole new look to furniture you already have. Change the hardware and knobs on cabinets, dressers, bedside tables, and desks. Switch out light plates, replace a faucet, buy sandpaper to scuff up old painted furniture to create a weathered look. The local hardware store also often has coupons and loyalty programs to save even more.

- **Online home design furniture sites:** If you search online for best bargain home décor websites you will find dozens of sites for any style of furniture you like. Places like Waverly.com, Joss & Main, and LexMod offer thousands of home decorating options for considerably less than retail stores. Many of these sites also have blogs with professional advice about common design trends and challenges.

- **Virtual design help:** Sometimes it actually pays to hire a professional to help. Thanks to the internet you can find reasonably priced help from professional designers online. Sites like Modsy.com will look at pictures of your rooms and help you create the look you want.

- **Google "decorating hacks":** The new meaning of "hack" when it comes to decorating is a simple solution, tip, or workaround. Hacks are the ultimate in DIY projects and you will be amazed by the clever, creative, and inexpensive ideas bloggers and design sites feature. You'll find ingenious cost saving ideas for any kind of decorating or any DIY project you can imagine by searching online.

Home Office

Since so many people are working from home these days, they're finding it doesn't take much room to create an office space. You can take the corner of a room, the space under a staircase, or a former closet and turn it into a work area. Search for small space offices online to find ideas that are big on efficiency even when you are short on space.

One of the best places to find bargains on office furniture is to check out your local county surplus warehouse. These stores sell used government office equipment. Chairs, desks, file cabinets, calculators, lamps — just about everything you would ever need in an office, and at low prices. When I originally did the story about county surplus warehouses, I was able to find a desk, chair, computer, calculator, and file cabinet for less than

$160. If you are part of a non-profit organization, you may be able to get all of the furniture for free.

Create an Outside Room

You can add an extra room to your house by creating a patio or garden area outdoors. And it doesn't have to break the bank. Like all of our other ideas, creating a low-cost yet magical space requires some planning. Check out your local nurseries and home improvement stores for how-to classes. For example, Lowe's has dozens of DIY workshops on everything from how to build a storage box to how to build arbors. Check your local stores to see what is offered in your area. Whether your potential patio space is a tiny balcony or a big backyard, you can be chilling outside in no time. If you don't have a patio already, you can create one inexpensively using a wide range of materials. Often times stores are happy to see these excess items put to good use. Here are a few ideas to start with.

- **Pallets:** Free pallets are a great resource for DIY projects like a simple deck. Not all pallets are free. You must ask the business owner before helping yourself. Pet food stores, liquor stores, flooring stores, and construction sites are good places to start. You may be able to also buy used pallets from home improvement stores or search for them on Craigslist. Search for online plans for decks, fencing, furniture, and more.

- **Gravel:** It's not free, but digging out the grass in a patio area and covering it with gravel can create a wonderful space for outdoor gatherings. Plus, gravel is less expensive to maintain than grass.

- **Found objects:** Discarded bricks, tiles, or other hardscape materials can make eclectic and beautiful homemade patios. You can find these for free on Craigslist, Freecycle, and for a low cost at Habitat for Humanity Restores. You dig out the grass, add a layer of sand, then place the hardscape over it. You can find all kinds of DIY info online for this project.

Patio Upgrade

If you have a deck or patio and it's looking a little faded around the edges, you can create a whole new look and feel by spending some time with these easy to access resources.

- **Paint:** Freshen up wood or concrete decks with paint. You can find hundreds of creative paint schemes, patterns, and stencils for patios online. Make sure you follow directions on how to clean and prep the surface first.

- **Lights:** Hang strings of lights to the patio area. Include them in potted plants, hang them from trellises, and fences. Inexpensive, battery operated lights can be attached to almost any pot, table, and railing.

- **Add a water feature:** You can make a fountain out of almost anything with an inexpensive solar hardware store pump. Bowls, pots, pottery saucers, tin buckets — there are dozens of ideas online. These can provide a soothing water sound for a patio, as well as a life-saving feature for birds and butterflies in your neighborhood.

- **Outdoor eating:** You don't need expensive patio furniture to create a quaint outdoor dining area. You can repurpose tables and chairs that you have, or create something new out of found materials. Just make sure it can be moved out of the rain if it's not made from outdoor-friendly materials. Make sure the outdoor furniture is sturdy. You don't want your guests tipping over at your parties.

Prune Plant Prices

You don't have to have a green thumb to experience the bounty of benefits gardening provides. Whether you till the back 40 or have a simple window sill herb patch, gardening improves health in a variety of ways; physically, mentally - and with a little know-how financially. It's one of those hobbies that can be practiced for next to nothing or make a big dent in your cost of living. I like to avoid high price tags at all costs, so here are some tried-and-true methods that I've picked up over the years, with the help of viewers and friends.

Soil is where it all starts, so it pays to take a little time to make sure yours has what it takes to support your plants, shrubs, and trees. Many communities give away free compost at the local waste and recycling centers. Or you can compost food waste from your family in a compost bin. Some communities provide these bins free or for a low cost. You can get free mulch from tree trimmers, who often are happy to deliver it at no charge. You can also buy soil amendments at gardening centers. Keep an eye out for discounts and coupons. You'll find a range of garden discounts in the most popular planting months in your area. If you do purchase flowers and plants, save the containers and your receipts. Some larger home stores offer an exchange policy if the plants or flowers don't survive.

Seeds, Cuttings, Volunteers

I have a friend who has a beautiful, thriving garden with dozens and dozens of varieties of plants, shrubs, and trees. Her garden delights the whole neighborhood, and is providing a welcome oasis to birds, bees, and butterflies. She has bought fewer than 10 plants for her front, back, and side yards. She's been the happy recipient of cuttings, seeds, and starts from friends and neighbors who know her passion and are happy to share. She does the same for others as well. Here's the method she uses.

- **Seed Libraries:** In the Bay Area we have many "libraries" where people can borrow seeds, plant them at home, then bring back more seeds after harvest. Many of these seed libraries are located in the main library and run by volunteers. Most of the seeds are for vegetables, but some libraries also have flower seed. Seed libraries are not only a great way to grow crops that will thrive in your area, they also provide a great place to meet other enthusiastic gardeners.

- **Starting from seed:** A few months or even weeks before the growing season, she gets out egg cartons and other recycled containers to start seeds for the garden. Some of these she buys, others are saved from last year's tomatoes and flowers. She lives in a warm climate so the seeds get started right on the patio. If you live in a colder location, you can start seeds inside.

- **Sharing:** My friend belongs to neighborhood social media communities like Nextdoor, where gardeners offer to swap and share seeds, starts, and cuttings. Some plants like succulents can be planted straight into the ground after being snapped off the original plant. So easy!

- **Stick with perennials:** Annuals need to be replanted every year. Perennials grow and grow, and when they get large enough, you can dig them up and divide them into multiple plants.

Vegetable Gardening on the Cheap

There are few things more satisfying than eating a meal made from food you grow yourself. As a country we could benefit by adding more healthy fruits and vegetables to our diets. Children who grow their own vegetables are more likely to be happy to try them and learn to like eating them. And backyard vegetable gardens can go far beyond a recreational activity. A few tomato plants can supply enough to make gallons and gallons of tomato sauce which can be frozen or canned. I have an Italian friend whose six-tomato plant harvest keeps the family in sauce for a whole year, and that's after eating and giving away at least half of the fresh crop. With cans of high-quality tomato sauce in the $5-plus range, she saves hundreds of dollars a year, and she feels the quality is much better.

If you don't have space in your yard for a garden, check to see if your neighborhood has a community garden you can use. These gardens usually are maintained by local residents who each get a small plot to plant. Everyone helps with the upkeep. It's a great way to meet your neighbors and grow healthy food at the same time.

The easiest crops to grow tend to be the ones people also love to put on their dinner tables. For me this includes tomatoes, squash, and green beans. This not only saves money, but having extra food to store and share with others is especially comforting in times of shortage and financial uncertainty.

Helping Others

Gardens can be a great source of giving back. The beauty of a nice landscape benefits everyone. Who doesn't love to get a basket of lemons, apples, or tomatoes from a friend's yard? And backyard gardens even feed communities in need.

In the Bay Area city of Albany, gardeners harvest excess fruit from trees for donation to the local food pantry and youth groups. The homeowner doesn't have to worry about unused fruit rotting on the ground and drawing pests. The volunteers get the great feeling of helping out, and the non-profit clients love being able to choose from the summer bounty of fresh produce.

For many of them, it's a rare treat they seldom get to enjoy. So dig into gardening. It really is a better way to save!

10. WINNING WARDROBES

Growing up in a family of five, my siblings and I were no strangers to hand-me-downs, and being the youngest, I had plenty! When we got a hole in our jeans, my mother would put a patch on them to make them last longer. Never in a million years would we have thought that someday people would actually pay $200 for jeans that were ripped. In our house, we had plenty of what we needed but nothing extravagant. My mother wore the same winter coat for 13 years. My dad had a dress belt and an everyday belt. When I would ask him why he wouldn't buy another belt he would say, "This one still holds my pants up. Why do I need two?" He had a point. That belt still sits curled on my desk to this day, a testament to my dad's practical frugality that I learned to admire with time.

When I wasn't wearing hand-me downs, I was wearing a lot of clothes my mother made for me. I loved going to the fabric store where mom and I would look through pattern books, pick out fabric, and carefully choose the right color thread. At home I would watch her sew. I sat in awe as she created my little designer outfits. In those days, this was one sure way to save money on clothes. And this is true today. But these days we have so many other ways to save on a wardrobe that weren't available then.

One memory from our era of sewing together stands out. Not only because I loved the clothes my mother sewed for me, but because there was a life lesson that came along with it. My kindergarten teacher asked each child to bring in an apron for paint class. I was so excited when my mom said she would make a brand-new apron just for me, not a hand-me-down. We picked out a fabric with small flowers and a simple, pretty trim. I can remember the day I brought my apron to class. We all put our aprons in a big box and then I counted the minutes until art class so I could debut my new frock. The clock finally ticked to the time to start painting and to my horror, my teacher told us to grab an apron and not to worry if it was the one we brought or not. I wouldn't get to wear my new, prized possession. I sat at my desk and cried. My teacher consoled me and explained that she hadn't realized my apron was so special to me and she just wanted everyone to share. If memory serves me, we made a deal that this time my classmate could use mine and next time I would have my apron. She was a very kind teacher and I learned a lot of lessons that day. My mother's beautiful work was a hit as fellow classmates ooh'd and ahh'd over it. I didn't need to be the model to appreciate how lovely my handmade apron was.

In the '60s and '70s, garment manufacturing was still a big business in the U.S. and in a big city like San Francisco, we were lucky to have many clothing outlets to choose from. We would head to the outlets for special occasion clothes. For my Winter Ball one year we hit the Gunny Sack Outlet where I bought a beautiful gown for $15. That was still a lot of money for my parents back then, but it was sure better than paying retail.

When I started earning money, I went a bit overboard on clothes, shoes, and yes, belts. I believed that some deals were too good to turn down, whether I had the money or not. When I didn't have the money, I reached for my credit card so I wouldn't miss out on the deal. I found my closet filled with clothes that still had their super low-cost sale price tags on them. I wasn't even wearing these irresistible finds. The "deals" evaporated as interest costs accrued when my credit card bills weren't paid in full at the end of each month. That interest added up. It was money that would have been better spent on items that I would love, even at twice the cost. I still get a twinge of regret when I think of the waste: the clothes I didn't wear, the interest fees I paid, and the true savings I missed out on - the ones that could have been in a savings account instead of my closet. It was a long time before I took a lesson from my friend, designer, celebrated author, and lifestyle expert, Lawrence Zarian who says "The best fashion statement is confidence! It's free and it will never go out of style. Embrace and celebrate who you are and only surround yourself with people who embrace and celebrate you for glorious YOU!" Only buying the things you really love will save you money AND time!

Whether you love to shop or not, most of us enjoy new clothes. And whether you're a fashionista or you wear a uniform to work, we all need new clothes from time to time. Your hard-working budget will heave a sigh of relief if there is a method to your clothes shopping madness. Fortunately, as with grocery shopping, what we spend on our wardrobe falls into our flexible monthly budget, the part we have some control over.

Ideally, what I like to do is take a look at what I have and clear out what I'm not using. That means scheduling an inventory of my closets regularly. My friends, family, and local charity thrift stores are all happy to get my gently used threads. I have even earned a few extra dollars by selling higher-end items at my local consignment shop. After you make room in your closet, the next step is to make a list of everything you need to pull your wardrobe together. My mom was big on mixing and matching pieces, which is actually a great idea if you are on a budget. Think colors and styles that work together to create several outfits. You should complete these steps before you even think about hitting a store. Once I know what I need and/or want, I use these strategies outlined below to make sure I'm not wasting money. And if I find something online that is not on my list, but I absolutely *must* have, I *try* to wait at least 24 hours before making the purchase. (Full disclosure, I'm still not perfect at this, lol) Let's go shopping!

The Price of Fast Fashion

Throwaway fashion may seem cheap, but it takes a toll on workers and the environment. There have been many news reports over the past several years showing ultra-cheap clothes are often made in sweat shops in third world countries, where workers are forced to work in terrible conditions for very little pay. And then there's the environmental cost. According to the Environmental Protection Agency, the average American throws away about 81 pounds of clothing every year. That adds more than 20 billion pounds of textile waste to landfills annually. And only about 15% of donated clothing actually ends up in the second-hand market. If you can find a way to use what you have and borrow or rent what you don't own, you will be helping your budget and the world.

Buying Clothes

The average American household spends nearly $1,900 annually on clothing and related services like cleaning and tailoring. That's about $160 per month. For many of us, this number is considerably higher especially if you are required to wear business suits to work. But you will be amazed how much you can strip off your clothing costs if you follow some of my favorite tips.

Taking Inventory

As I mentioned, I try to go through closets regularly, at least once every six months. To make sure this happens, schedule it on your calendar. If you haven't worn something in six months, either decide to remove it or move it to a place where you'll see it more easily. If you still haven't used it when the next clean-up day rolls around, it's time to let it go. This rule basically applies to your everyday wardrobe, not special occasion or business suits. Make sure clothes have all their buttons, the zippers work, and are clean. Do the same with your shoes and every once in a while, do it for accessories. This not only keeps your space organized and clutter-free, it reminds you what you have on hand and what you need. Often times I will find items that I completely forgot about that I really love. It's like going shopping in my own closet.

Use What You Own

The least expensive wardrobe is the one you already own. Here are some good ways to stretch what you have, and a strategy to add to your wardrobe intentionally.

Capsule Wardrobes

One of the most transformational concepts to hit the fashion world in the past 50 years is the capsule wardrobe. The brainchild of London boutique owner extraordinaire Susie Faux more than 40 years ago. Faux saw her clients waste time and money on ill-fitting clothes made of poor-quality materials that sat unused in clogged closets. She counseled her clients to build a whole wardrobe around a fixed number of classic, well-made pieces that can be accessorized for multiple occasions. Faux's original idea was that between 30 and 40 items should be enough clothing to mix and match for dozens of different outfits. The idea really took off in the '80s with Donna Karan's *Seven Easy Pieces* collection. Made up of pieces like the LBD (Little Black Dress), classic black blazer, pants, and skirt, the same pieces could be accessorized for almost any occasion. Most of the key or staple items are in coordinating colors.

In the years that followed, budget-minded fashionistas have personalized the concept and the number of pieces that qualify as a capsule. You can find capsules for 12 pieces that create 30 or 40 different outfits. You can find ideas for capsule wardrobes for any occasion and for any budget. The benefits of creating a capsule wardrobe are many:

- **Less stress**: You don't have to worry about what to wear.

- **More time:** Choosing an outfit is much easier.

- **Less clutter**: A streamlined closet feels much better than a clogged one.

- **More style**: Once you focus on well-made clothes that fit well and that you love, you will exude a new sense of style.

- **More savings**: You won't be wasting money on clothes you don't wear. Quality clothes don't need replacement as often.

- **Less landfill**: What's good for your wallet is good for the planet. Americans are dumping 20 billion pounds of textile waste a year in landfills. In this case, less is more.

Where to Start?

Luckily, there is a capsule wardrobe for every season, style, and spending plan. And it's easy to find inspiration and guidance online by searching sites like Instagram, Pinterest, and Etsy. There are some specific tools that make putting capsule wardrobes together a snap. Here are some of my favorites.

Templates

Search capsule wardrobe templates online for basic templates you can print out. Use the templates to inventory your closet and then take them shopping with you to fill in any gaps. A template can be inspiration to help you to use pieces you already have as building blocks, and to make a list to intentionally add others. Templates can also be a great source of inspiration.

Apps

There are an amazing number of apps that will help you pull together a wardrobe from your own closet or by adding a few pieces here and there. These are some of my favorites.

- **Cladwell:** First up, the Cladwell app, which lets you upload your own clothing or choose images that are similar to what you have. The app then creates basic wardrobes, seasonal capsules, and special occasion outfits for you. With Cladwell you can use 100% of your own wardrobe to create different outfits. This app also takes the weather into account when suggesting daily outfits, which can be a real plus. Cladwell is incredibly easy to use and doesn't take a lot of time to set up. The stylists make many suggestions that are easy to visualize and follow. The app allows you to try it free for a week before choosing a plan, and then there is a monthly subscription fee. Be sure to check for promotions like a year's subscription for half-off from time to time. If you want to be able to build wardrobes using clothes you already own, with great suggestions, this might be the app for you.

- **Stylebook:** The Stylebook app wants you to get the most out of what you have in your closet, and to choose new pieces that integrate well into your wardrobe as a whole. Not only does the app keep track of your style, it keeps track of the cost of your style, by having you add the prices of your garments when you upload them. Was that $200 pencil skirt really worth the price when you've worn it exactly once in four years? Stylebook tracks your statistics, so you know how often you actually wear each outfit. You can also easily shop for specific items using this app. Stylebook charges a one-time fee in the app store. Users say it's definitely worth the price of a latte to get a handle on streamlining your closet, and getting a snapshot on what unplanned shopping trips are costing you.

- **Other apps:** Cladwell and Stylebook are the two of the most popular wardrobe planning tools out there right now, but there are many more on the market. Like with most technology, everyone has a style they are most comfortable with. It's worth doing a little research to find the app you like best. You could find yourself saving a considerable chunk of change when you stop buying clothes you don't love and won't use. On the upside, these apps make it easy to look marvelous every day.

Accessorize

You can get more mileage out of the same outfit by changing your jewelry, scarf, sweater, or shoes. You can get inspiration by searching for capsule wardrobes online. And another tip from Lawrence Zarian, "Whether it's a necklace, scarf, or bag, choose to invest in that one piece that always makes you feel… pretty, sexy, hot, amazing! And don't forget, a smile is that one accessory that goes with absolutely everything!"

Clothing Swaps

Years ago, I did a fun, feel-good story on Clothing Swap and its fabulous founder Suzanne Agasi. Suzanne came up with a brilliant idea to help women lose the clothes they no longer use, find wardrobe pieces they love, and help a well deserving charity along the way. Her motto: "Be Good. Be Green. Be Glam." Suzanne has hosted over 300 of these swaps. We filmed the story at a local nightclub in San Francisco. For a minimal entrance fee, the shoppers were pampered with tasty treats and swag bags, not to mention the new clothes. The profits from the entrance fees went toward the charity of the evening. Women arrived with their "pre-loved" bag of clothes and accessories in hand. Everything was set up on racks and shelves. At about 8 o'clock, there was a countdown and you heard "Ladies, let's go!" Women had so much fun finding items they loved to add to their wardrobe. Anything that was left was donated to a local women's shelter. It was an amazing evening and everyone left happily with their new wardrobe items in hand.

You can host an event like this with your friends at home. Organize your swap by inviting friends over for a specific amount of time (you can do a lot of swapping in two hours!) Have your friends bring a bag of gently used clothes. Just set aside a space in your home and decide how to organize the items. For example, use the dining room table for sweaters, clothes racks for dresses and coats, and the couch for pants and shorts. Shoes can go up against the wall. Don't limit the swap to clothes. Have people include jewelry and accessories, too. Start the swap with a short preview time, where everyone gets a look at what's available. Donate any items left to your local charitable thrift store. It's a great way to get and give at the same time.

When You Need Something New or Just New to You

My first news story at our local station was on how to put together your child's wardrobe on a budget. I was able to create an entire child's wardrobe for around $100. Many years later I did a similar segment for Hallmark's Home & Family Show. That time I showed a wardrobe for a family of four for $400. The wardrobe went from pajamas to dress clothes and included everything in between. I accomplished this feat by shopping for most of the items at resale and consignment shops. If you aren't familiar with these stores, they are a really brilliant idea and they've come a long way from the second-hand stores of my childhood. Customers bring gently used clothes to the store. Once the shop sells the items, the customer gets a portion of the money or a credit to the store. It's a great way to make money, save money, and help the environment. Some of the best deals I have ever found have been in kids' resale shops. Kids, especially babies, often grow out of their clothes before they are really even used. You can even find clothes with the original price tags still on them sometimes.

Let's take a look at some places you can save a significant amount of money on for all types of clothes for the entire family. If you don't own it and can't borrow it, these are for you.

- **Consignment stores:** Since Marie Kondo made decluttering a religion of sorts, brick-and-mortar or online stores like Poshmark, Thred Up, Kidizen, Plato's Closet, and Uptown Cheapskate are treasure troves for everyday fashion and designer threads, too. Just like any store, they have regular sales and promotions, so try to double up on savings opportunities. And you can bring a bag of very gently used clothes with you to sell at the same time. Check their websites before you head out for coupons and promotions.

- **Luxury consignment:** Sites like the RealReal and Vestiaire Collective have shockingly low prices on gently used high-end brands like Prada, Christian Dior, and Chanel to name just a few. These sites are known for their commitment to authenticity. They have teams of experts who examine every item they sell. This is important because luxury brand counterfeits abound. (More on that later.) These sites are also good ways to earn money if you have designer items you don't use. You can also find amazing brick-and-mortar, high-end consignment shops. One smart tip is to search for consignment shops in affluent areas. For example, in San Francisco I would often frequent a lovely shop in the Pacific Heights neighborhood. I found amazing deals on clothes that someone may have worn once to an event and then turned it in for resale. Resale shops run by non-profits like the Junior League and Hospice also usually carry designer clothes and accessories. I found a beautiful St. John knit suit near my neighborhood at The American Cancer Society thrift store for $125. I wore that suit for years!

- **Social media consignment groups:** Fashion forward stores and entrepreneurs have had great success founding groups that cater to buyers and sellers on Facebook and Instagram. Once you are accepted into the group, you have access to all of the site's sales and discussions. If you're a W Stitch Fix member, for example, you can buy and sell from the W Stitch Fix B/S/T Facebook group that has 50,000 plus members buying, selling, and trading Stitch Fix clothes. Do a little digging on your own and you will find many consignment groups that fit your tastes.

- **Shop sales:** Like grocery stores, your favorite clothing stores also have reward programs, promotions, and sales. Make sure you have alerts set up to receive the news. You hold items in your cart and wait for the sales and promotions before you buy. But if it is something that is a must have, you may want to get it right away so you don't risk the item being sold out.

- **Bidding sites**: eBay auctions are a great place to shop designer duds, handbags, and shoes. I once scored a Prada purse for about a hundred dollars.

- **Coupons:** Sign up for coupons from your favorite stores and scour the internet for better deals on sale items.

- **Use your calendar:** For nearly 10 years, I have been writing a monthly Best Buys column. You'll find great deals on everything swimwear right after the 4th of July and even better deals after Labor Day. Winter coats are deeply discounted in January and marked to clear out what's left by March. If you have your list ready you can scoop up a great deal on items you are holding in your cart. Be sure to check my Monthly Best Buys Chapter for a complete list of what to buy when.

- **Thrift stores:** Get to know the people at your local thrift store. You may be able to cut hours off scouring the racks if the sales clerks know you and know what you like. Shop on their tag days — usually one day a week or month when everything with a tag is either marked down or Buy One, Get One.

- **Budget basics:** There's no reason to spend top dollar on tank tops, t-shirts, and workout gear. You can find great, classic staples in the latest colors at stores like Ross, Marshalls, and other off-price or surplus stores. You will also find deals on underwear, bras, socks, and nightwear. Follow discount stores' social media accounts to find out about upcoming deals. And be sure to check the clearance racks.

- **Check out the men's and kids' departments:** Women's clothing often sports pricier tags than men's or kids'. If you are looking for basics such as hoodies, T-shirts, and shorts you can find good deals here.

- **Rent:** Most people don't have closets full of formal wear and if you only need a tux or evening gown once a decade, it makes sense to rent. But you would be surprised how much formal wear is available online and in consignment stores. Don't assume renting is the cheapest way to go.

- **Price adjustments:** Price adjustments are one of my favorite money saving tips of all-time. With a price adjustment, you can spend money now and save it later. If you buy something and it goes down in price within a certain period of time (usually 14 days), you can get the difference between what you paid and the new, lower price back. All you need to do is save your receipt. Most major department stores have a price adjustment policy. You can also use these adjustments when shopping online. I have saved thousands over my lifetime by doing this one thing.

- **Sewing:** As I mentioned at the beginning of this chapter, my mother saved our family hundreds of dollars by sewing clothes for us. If you have a sewing machine and a little know-how, you can do the same.

Making Clothes Stand the Test of Time

- **Consider cleaning:** Machine washable is the way to go. Think twice before buying fabrics that need dry cleaning. Cashmere or silk on sale is no bargain if you are paying $5 every time you clean it. If you do opt for a dry-clean-only label, make sure to check out Consumer Checkbook's ratings in your area for the best service and prices. At home dry cleaning kits run about $10 and usually wash about 16 average size items. Keep in mind, these kits aren't right for all fabrics. And don't forget to consider upkeep costs when buying clothes with sequins, beads, or many pleats, which all require special care and attention. Dry cleaning and pressing costs can transform a bargain into a pricey purchase in no time.

- **Take care of your clothes:** Use the gentle cycle with cool water for washing and consider line drying to get the maximum wear from your clothes. Zippers should always be zipped for washing and drying. In the closet or drawers, remove plastic dry-cleaning bags, hang your clothes, and don't over- stuff drawers.

- **Add some sole to your shoes:** I have some shoes that I have resoled 2 or 3 times. It is a fabulous way to hold onto your comfy, broken-in shoes and save a lot of money. I have a local shoemaker that does an amazing job. He also can repair shoes that might be coming apart at the seams. As I slip my feet into them they feel like a new, comfy pair of shoes.

- **Clothes that don't fit:** Don't buy anything unless you can wear it now. There will be more sales when you lose that extra five pounds.

Buyer Beware

During my eight years writing my *Buyer Beware* column for *MarketWatch*, I was always amazed by how strategic some marketers were in separating consumers from their cash. Most of us have weaknesses when it comes to shopping and can easily be swayed. Here are some typical problem areas for bargain hunters.

- **Sales:** If you buy things you don't need and won't use, it doesn't matter how much money you are theoretically saving. You are actually throwing your money away. Create some safety rails for tempting situations. Some tried-and-true methods: shop with a list only, wait 24 hours before making purchases not on the list, and shop with cash. Ask yourself if you will really use the new item, or if there is already something similar in your closet.

- **Opening store credit cards:** Retailers often offer a special discount to your purchase if you open their store credit card. This can be helpful if you have a large purchase but you *must* be able to pay the entire balance off before the due date. Otherwise, you really aren't saving anything. Some promotions will allow you to delay payment for, say, three months. Read the fine print. If you are one day late, you may be responsible for all of the interest for that entire three-month period.

- **Outlet stores:** Outlet stores are usually destination shopping experiences, where you spend the day going through a dozen stores or more, all with sales tags screaming BUY ME! BUY ME! Though the outlet store may have a high-end name, there is no guarantee that they carry the same products sold in the regular stores. Reams of research show that outlet retailers regularly manufacture a different quality of goods to be sold at outlets. Often, the "Compare At" price tags claim what the item would cost at a typical "full price" store. See more about Outlet Shopping Warnings by the Federal Trade Commission at the end of this chapter. That said, you can find some really great deals at outlet malls. The best days to shop for deals are Tuesday, Wednesday, and Thursday. Shop early in the day to avoid the after-lunch crush. Before arriving, check on the outlet mall's website for VIP coupons and perks. I once did a story on outlet mall deals. At the time, if you went to the mall's main office you could pick up a 10% VIP discount card.

- **Fakes:** Counterfeiters are really good at what they do these days, and when it comes to fake fashion, they find an enthusiastic market on social media platforms. Fakers are especially drawn to sites where content disappears. The sale of fakes doesn't just hurt brand integrity or profits of the name brand; counterfeits have been linked to funding terrorism and other criminal activity. It can be extremely hard to tell the real from the fake.

Here are some tips to make sure the luxury items you buy on sale are the real deal.

- If it seems too good to be true, it is. Period. The chances that someone is selling thousands of cut-rate luxury items at once are slim to none. Don't fall for these tantalizing teases.

- Read the seller's profile and compare it to the official website of the brand you want to buy. If the seller's website is written with poor grammar or has other glaring design flaws beware. Know who you are buying from.

- Research the sellers online. You can often find numerous warnings and red flags about unscrupulous sellers. Check with the manufacturer to see if the seller is legitimate.

Helping Others

This is one area where we can really pay it forward without spending a dime. Donating clothes that you are no longer using can make a significant difference in the lives of so many people. Business attire is especially helpful for people as they enter the workplace. Organizations such as Dress for Success put together a wardrobe including accessories for women once they have a job interview. There are similar programs available for men. It is a big confidence booster to be able to arrive at an interview with a completely new outfit. There are variations on the "Dress for Success" theme in communities across the country. You can do a little legwork to find some near you.

Or, combine your purchasing with giving to those in need by purchasing from a social enterprise business that helps the poor, or people rebuilding their lives, such as jewelry from Her Future Coalition or accessories from Ten Thousand Villages.

11. MAN'S BEST FRIEND

Puccini Pavini: How I Became a Dog Lover

When I was growing up, we didn't have a dog because it was challenging enough for my parents to afford to feed and care for five kids. I did have two turtles, though, and I loved them. I named them Mike (after my brother-in-law who bought him for me) and Stiches (named after the 12 stiches I got when I split open my chin and "Stiches" was a get-well gift). I would sit and play my records and sing to Stiches and Mike for hours. There is something so comforting with any type of pet. In 2018, I rescued my first dog. I was hesitant and really had no idea what to expect. Little did I know that I would fall in love. His name is Puccini Pavini and he has become a very important member of our family. And like caring for any member of a family, there are responsibilities and expenses. I also feel pets can be a great source of therapy that doesn't cost a dime. The comfort and calm petting an animal brings is worth a lot to our sanity. While I have been writing this entire book, Puccini has either been at my feet or on my lap. Additionally, dogs force us to get out and walk which is always good for both our physical and mental health. Puccini is also very popular with the neighbors. We have lived in our house for many years, yet we barely knew any of the people in our neighborhood. Because of our daily walks, we now know everyone and their dogs! It's harder for me to wake up on the wrong side of the bed when I have a 20-pound cutie pie wagging his tail and jumping in the air because he sees me.

Dime-a-dozen goldfish, hamsters, turtles, cuddly kittens, pricey Pomeranians - we love our pets in the U.S. More than two-thirds of American households own an animal. The cost of owning a pet extends beyond food, water, and shelter. The ASPCA estimates the first-year costs of owning a dog averages $1,000. Fortunately, it doesn't have to be that way. The ways to save on your pet are endless. Here are some of my favorite tips.

The Cost of Owning a Pet

There is no doubt that while the joy animals bring to a household can be priceless, responsible pet ownership *does* have a price tag. The average cost of care for our furry family member can significantly increase if your pet needs medical care or has special needs.

The ASPCA calculates the average lifetime price tags in its annual "Pet Care Costs" Survey:

- Small dog: $15,051 (average life expectancy of 15 years)

- Medium dog: $15,782 (average life expectancy of 13 years)

- Large dog: $14,480 (average life expectancy of 10 years)

- Cat: $11,000 (12 years with no emergency medical treatment)

If you can't afford to comfortably pay your pet's food and medical bills, it may be better to pet sit or foster a pet instead. Shelters are full of heartbroken animals whose owners can't afford them anymore. That said, there are many ways to considerably lower the costs of pet ownership. Let's get back to basics with some strategies to stay within your means!

Bringing Home Baby - Shelters

No matter what kind of pet you have your heart set on, chances are you can find it through an animal shelter or rescue organization. There definitely isn't a shortage of animals in need of a home in this country. According to the ASPCA, each year approximately 1.5 million shelter animals in the U.S. are euthanized (670,000 dogs and 860,000 cats). We are doing better than we have in previous years as shelters have been more successful at reuniting lost animals with their owners and adopting out the rest. But we still have a long way to go. When you adopt a shelter animal your pet will have been spayed or neutered and brought up-to-date on shots. Many shelters throw in little extras as well. When we adopted Puccini, we got a free month of pet insurance as a gift from the rescue organization.

When you adopt from a shelter, you are not only saving money, you're saving a life. I know from personal experience, that the gratitude you feel from your rescued pet is real. It is an amazing feeling. In many ways your new companion rescues you as well.

Rescue Organizations

If you have your heart set on that Golden Doodle or Maine Coon Cat, you can save a bundle by adopting from a rescue organization. These mostly volunteer groups rescue specific breeds when they're surrendered to shelters. There are adoption costs but they are far lower than it would cost to purchase from a breeder. Some organizations run adoption events where they will waive certain fees. I realize when adopting a rescue animal there might be unknown behavioral concerns. If, for some reason, after working with your pet the adoption doesn't work out, many rescue groups will allow you to bring back your pet. In fact, the organization we rescued from asked that if for any reason we no longer wanted to keep our dog that we bring him directly back to them. Fortunately, Puccini was my dream dog and it has been one of the best experiences of my life.

Another advantage of working with a local rescue group, be it a breed-specific or all-breed rescue, is that usually when the organization receives the animal they will do a thorough health check, a temperament test, provide emergency veterinary care, and observe the animal in foster care. This will help them to match you with the pet that's right for your lifestyle.

Fostering

Rescue organizations and shelters often need people to foster animals while they're waiting for their forever home. This is also a good way for potential pet owners to get to know an animal which they may end up adopting. The organizations often pay for food and medical care of the foster animals.

Training

Behavior problems are the most common reason that people surrender dogs to animal shelters, and the second most common reason for cats. These problems can range from annoyances like house-training accidents to more serious behaviors such as aggression, biting, or fighting with other animals. Many behavior problems can be handled with training and happily there are many low-cost options to meet your training needs. Here are some places to look.

- **Online help:** If your pet has a common problem you can find specific videos geared toward the exact behavior you want to change. Some trainers also offer one-on-one sessions online for considerably less than what you would pay a trainer in person. This option is great if you live in an area without a lot of local options.

- **Community centers, local SPCA or Humane Society branches, dog clubs:** You can find low cost training programs in your community.

- **Pet supply stores:** Many larger chain pet stores offer low-cost group classes for dogs and owners. This is a good way for both pets and their owners to learn techniques for conquering common behavioral issues. These classes are also an excellent way to socialize your new four-legged friend, bond with them, and meet new friends.

Food and Medication

Food is usually the biggest ongoing expense of owning a pet, but saving money by purchasing low quality food might not be a bargain. It's important to understand the nutritional needs of your pet and know how to read pet food labels. Low quality food may put an animal's long-term health at risk and will end up costing you more in vet bills. Good quality dog food typically runs between $20 and $60 a month depending on the size and energy level of your dog. Cat food ranges from very affordable to very expensive and averages between $7.50 and $210 per month. The labeling of pet food doesn't necessarily relate to the nutritional value. It is important to know the specific ingredients in your pet food. Pets with problems like sensitive skin, digestive issues, or obesity might do better on special food, so talk with your vet. Even in those cases, you'll find significant price differences in the choices available.

• **Portion control**: One important way to save money is to avoid over-feeding your pet. Obesity in pets leads to health problems like diabetes, arthritis, and cancer. That can add up to some big vet bills and bigger heartache. I know from my experience with Puccini that it's easy to overfeed a dog. I ended up wasting food and money, and I don't like wasting either of those things!

Ways to Save on Food

- **Online:** Some vets recommend you stick with one brand of pet food, as it helps keep digestive problems at bay. This makes it easy to shop online for the best prices. Keep an eye out for promotions and coupons to bring low online prices even lower. Follow your favorite brands' social media for specific specials for their fans.

- **Big box stores:** Big box stores like Costco sell high quality foods under their own label at a price that's hard to beat. They also carry other brands with warehouse pricing to match. Costco also has great prices on flea medicine for both dogs and cats. You can also have your vet send your pet's prescriptions to Costco pharmacies, usually the prices are significantly lower.

- **Make your own:** I have done my own cost comparison and found that if I buy items such as chicken, rice, potatoes, and broth when it is on sale, making my own food is cost effective. The same money saving strategies I use for grocery shopping apply here: use your grocery store loyalty program to get the best deals for that week on items like meat and then use coupons to save more money. But be sure to talk to your vet before giving up on store-bought pet food. You want to make sure you meet your pet's nutritional needs.

- **Rewards programs:** Many pet stores offer rewards programs for food. For example, if you buy 10 bags you get one free. Most stores run weekly promotions as well on certain brands with a buy one-get one offer.

- **Buy in bulk:** Make sure you have a good, rodent-proof container for the open food bags. If you have room to store food, the best buys are often in bulk.

- **Feed stores:** Unless you live on a farm, you're probably not familiar with "Seed and Feeds." As a pet owner, it's worth it to check your local feed store for incredible savings on products that are packaged for horses but work for dogs and cats. You can find pine pellets packaged for horses for less than $10 for 40-pound bags. The exact same pine pellets, packaged for cat litter, costs the same $10, but you usually only get a 10-pound bag.

- **Subscription service:** Amazon and some online pet stores offer a discount when you set up an order for regular scheduled delivery.

- **Vet's office:** While the vet's office isn't usually the place to save on pet meds, you can ask for coupons and free samples of food and medicine.

- **Pharmacy:** You can ask your pharmacist to fill certain pet prescriptions, usually at considerable savings over what you would pay at the vet. Walgreens is just one of many commercial pharmacies now filling valid prescriptions from veterinarians. CVS pharmacies will fill a pet prescription if the drug is also prescribed for humans (many treatments for digestive troubles, itching, infections, and high blood pressure are the same). Walmart also has an online pet prescription service.

Healthcare

A healthy lifestyle leads to lower healthcare costs for people *and* animals. Make sure your pet eats a healthy diet and gets exercise. Protect your pet from harm by staying current with shots, vaccinations, and medications. Spay or neuter your pet. Keep dogs on a leash and cats inside to avoid accidents. Even the healthiest pets need to go to the vet's office from time to time. Here are a few ways to save.

• **Low cost and subsidized care:** Search out routine free and low-cost services in your community. Your local animal shelter will know where you can find low-cost rabies shots, spay and neuter clinics, and other services.

• **Promotions:** Look for vet office promotions in local papers and online.

• **Pet insurance:** Consumer Reports research shows pet insurance plans are one of the fastest growing optional perks being offered to employees, so it's worth checking your benefits to see if you can sign up. When it comes to the policies themselves, it's important to read them carefully and talk to your vet about the kinds of care your breed might need. Some policies exclude common breed-specific ailments like hip and heart problems. Research shows problems like cancer treatment can be worth the price of insurance. Some programs even include routine care. Most vets expect you to pay out of pocket and wait for reimbursement, but some vet offices will take payments directly from the insurer. Just make sure to check. I have done many news stories on the pros and cons of buying pet insurance. It can be a game-changer should there be a catastrophic accident or illness. Always check the policy for their disclaimers on pre-existing conditions. Many people start their policies when the animals are young to avoid being trapped by certain pre-existing condition clauses. Also, ask if there is a cap to how much the insurance company will pay per illness. There are some policies that do not have a cap which is a lifesaver for illnesses such as cancer.

•   **Drop-in vet visits:** Some of the larger pet store chains offer low-cost drop-in visits one day a week at the store's location. I have seen these visits for as low as $15.

•   **Veterinarian colleges:** If you live near a veterinarian college, you may be able to find low-cost or even free care. Graduate students who are about to begin their career need real animals to treat. These students are typically supervised by some of the best career veterinarians.

Grooming

Grooming costs can add up fast. Dog groomers typically charge extra for additional services such as teeth cleaning and nail clipping. On average, expect to pay between $30 and $90 for standard grooming, depending on the size of your pet and its amount of fur. There are plenty of ways to save on this service. Here are some of my favorites.

- **Coupons and promotions:** Check Groupon for groomers. They often offer deals to entice new clients.

- **Avoid peak grooming times:** Ask your groomer if you can save money by booking your appointment during less busy times.

- **Go for basic services:** Fancy cuts cost more.

- **Self-service grooming:** You can save money by bathing your pooch yourself at the self-service wash. Better yet, do it at home for free.

- **Stretch out appointments:** Instead of seeing the groomer every 6 weeks, see if you can stretch it out to 8 weeks.

- **Invest in wipes:** If you wipe down your pooch in between baths you can sometimes stretch out bath times.

- **Brush, brush, brush:** Regular brushing helps avoid a variety of problems, and it's a nice bonding time between you and your pet.

- **Do it yourself:** Like everything else, there are a variety of grooming videos online to help budding do-it-yourselfers learn how.

Everything Else

Pets can require a lot of gear. Dishes, leashes, beds, clothes, toys, fences — the list seems endless. Here are ways to keep even the most pampered pooch happy, without breaking the bank.

- **DIY toys:** Glean Pinterest, YouTube, and crafting sites for ideas.

- **Gently used products:** Goodwill, Freecycle, Craigslist, yard sales, and friends have things like crates, leashes, and puppy toys. Be sure to clean these before using them.

- **Make them last:** Don't give your dog access to his favorite toys all the time. Put them away and take them out for playtime.

- **Set a budget and stick to it:** If you have a habit of getting carried away buying pet toys or clothes, setting a budget will help you from running crazily off leash.

- **Shop smart:** Off-price and discount stores such as Marshalls and Ross have name-brand, quality pet beds, accessories, and toys at unbeatable prices.

Helping Others

Whether you own a pet or not, there are ways you can help our four- legged friends. Shelters are always looking for donations of clean towels, blankets, and sheets as well as office and cleaning supplies. Some shelters need volunteers to help care for the animals, walk them, or even just cuddle with them.

12. ON THE ROAD AGAIN

On their wedding night, Feb. 4, 1950, my father wanted to take my mother to one of San Francisco's finest establishments. He saved $10 so they could spend the night at the Palace Hotel. I still have the original receipt (yes, he saved it), it was $10.51, plus 10 cents for a phone call. The next morning, they put on their best traveling suits and took the train to Palm Springs. They couldn't afford a flight so they made the most of the budget they did have.

My dad and mom didn't have the resources we have today to save money on travel. They couldn't go online to compare prices to get the best deals on transportation, hotels, and restaurants. And although we have these online tools today, they don't ensure you are getting the best deal. If you were to ask the two people sitting next to you on your next flight about what they paid, you would find that the three of you paid three different prices. In fact, other people may have paid 30% less than you. The same goes for people staying in the hotel room right next to yours. One of you probably paid more. But there are ways to maximize the chances that you will be the traveler who pays the least.

The travel industry was devastated by coronavirus in 2020. Travel to many parts of the world has been impossible, as borders closed internationally. The pandemic highlighted cracks in consumer protections for travelers. Many found out the hard way that nonrefundable tickets live up to their names. Some waited months for refunds, while others had to be satisfied with vouchers that expire after a certain period of time. It was yet another wake-up call for consumers to understand the fine print. The travel industry is always changing, but never as much as it has as a result of the pandemic shutdown – and it continues to change. The industry is responding to current events day-by-day. Here are some post-pandemic changes that could help you feel more comfortable booking a trip in the future.

- **Change fees:** Almost all airlines are waiving change fees. Those are the fees the airlines charge when you make a change to an existing reservation. This may not last forever, so be sure to ask before you book.

- **Flexible rebooking:** Most airlines are offering more flexible rebooking rules by extending the length of time travelers can use the tickets from a canceled flight.

- **Refund issues:** Some airlines have made it more difficult to receive a refund instead of a voucher for canceled flights in the United States. Europe generally has passenger friendly cancellation policy rules, but make sure you check what they are before buying a ticket. I've heard from several people who have had problems receiving refunds for travel they won't be able to reschedule within a year.

- **Use miles:** For future trips, using miles is a great way to protect your investment and often cheaper than travel insurance. Travelers can usually redeposit miles within a few days of their travel dates. Some airlines, like Southwest, don't charge customers to cancel and redeposit their miles, others charge $50 to $200 a ticket for most travelers. While the change fees can add up, they still might be a better deal than trying to get a refund on an all-cash ticket.

While we are all still learning many valuable and very important lessons from the global pandemic of 2020, the road to economic and commercial recovery is shaping up to include some unique opportunities for the budget conscious traveler. It's a good idea to keep an eye on your favorite travel websites and bloggers for the latest updates.

Airfare

These days it's not just enough to compare the base cost of an airline ticket. You need to carefully consider all the extra fees airlines are charging for things like: baggage, seating, canceling or changing reservations, and more. In 2019, consumers were projected to be nickeled and dimed to the tune of $109.5 billion for ancillary fees, according to the IdeaWorksCompany.com, which has compiled the survey of fees for 10 years. Make sure you understand the fee structure and also the cancellation policies of any airline before paying for a ticket.

In addition to being aware of fees that add to your ticket price, here are some other tips to keep in mind when booking.

- **Sales start on Tuesdays:** Typically, airfare sales start on a Tuesday and can run for several days.

- **Fare wars:** When a sale is posted, wait until about 4 p.m. Eastern to see if other airlines have matched it or have brought their pricing down to be more competitive.

- **Day of the week:** The least expensive days to fly are usually Tuesdays and Wednesdays. Traveling on a Friday or Sunday can cost twice as much as other days.

- **Fly early:** If you want to avoid travel delays, aim for the earliest flight out. Avoid booking the last flight of the day, which could leave you delayed or stranded.

- **July can be pricey:** For summer flights, July can be the most expensive month to travel. If you wait until after mid-August you will find a significant savings on both airfare and hotels. Mid-April is usually when you will find the best rates for pre- booking your summer travel.

- **Travel insurance:** If you are buying travel insurance, you may want to consider using an independent travel insurance company. They usually offer good coverage and rates. Check with your credit card companies, auto club, and homeowners or renter's insurance to see what coverage they offer before you buy travel insurance. Additionally, read the fine print. Most people buy travel insurance in case they become ill and can't take the trip. But many of these policies have clauses such as proving the illness was not part of a pre- existing condition, which can sometimes be difficult to prove. In all my years of consumer reporting, issues with travel insurance coverage was a consistent complaint.

- **Upgrade 24 hours ahead:** Certain airlines offer inexpensive upgrades within 24 hours of your flight. If you have a lot of reward miles saved, check to see if you can use some miles for an upgrade.

- **Compare prices for nearby airports:** If you are flying out of or into an area with a couple of options for airports, be sure to compare prices. You can save a considerable amount of money by doing this one thing.

- **Use coupons, codes, and promotions:** When you are using a discount travel site to book your travel online, check to see if there is a coupon code available to give you an additional savings. Many times you can get an additional discount on top of their already low prices.

- **Loyalty programs**: If you do nothing else, make sure you take advantage of loyalty programs. Perks such as faster check-in, shorter security lines, upgraded seats, and miles towards future free travel make this a no-brainer. If you are going to have to travel, why not make it work for you?

- **Disable cookies:** Consider disabling your cookies on your computer before you search for airfares. Some research has suggested that some airlines use cookies to track your search activity; finding that if you check a price for airfare and leave the site only to come back to it later, the price may be higher. And at the same time you are being quoted a higher price, someone sitting right next to you could log on and find a price that's lower. I tried this and that is what happened.

Getting Bumped

Know the rules when it comes to getting bumped from a flight and it could actually work to your advantage. Keep in mind that every airline has their own check-in deadline and if you miss that you may lose your reservation and therefore any bumping compensation.

- **Arrive early:** Getting to the airport early is the best way to make sure you get on your flight. Even if an airline bumps by fare level, they will generally start with the lowest fare class and bump those who checked in last.

- **Volunteer:** Airlines will ask for volunteers before bumping unwilling passengers. Since airlines want happy customers, they will often up the ante to get volunteers before forcing someone to switch flights.

- **Ask the right questions:** Make sure you get a confirmed seat on the next flight, not a standby ticket. Overnight costs could negate your compensation. Be sure the airline will pay for your hotel and ground transportation in addition to giving you a voucher for future travel. There's room for negotiation, so ask for a seat upgrade or meal vouchers, especially if the airline is having a difficult time getting volunteers. Try to get a travel voucher for a certain dollar amount rather than "free" tickets, which usually have more restrictions.

Involuntary Bumping

With involuntary bumping, airlines must follow a strict set of compensation standards. These can change, but currently here are the rules they should play by.

- You are not entitled to any compensation if you get to your destination within an hour of the original arrival time.

- If you arrive within one to two hours (or one to four hours internationally), the airline must pay double your one-way fare, with a $650 maximum.

- If you arrive more than two hours later (or four hours internationally), the airline must pay you four times your one-way fare, with a $1,300 maximum.

- If you are involuntarily bumped, you have the right to insist on a check instead of a voucher or tickets.

Hotels

I have stayed in my fair share of hotels over the years. I have stayed in rooms that were a big disappointment and others that were a pleasant surprise. And although they never compare to the comfort of my own home (and bed), there are things you can do to make your stay the best it can be. Keep in mind that many mileage programs allow you to turn in miles for hotel stays. It may be worth it if you are finding it difficult to cash in those miles for flights.

- **Call the hotel directly:** When booking a room, call the hotel directly and you may have more room to negotiate. A chain's toll-free number is usually working off set rates.

- **Check online:** Often, the lowest price is an online special you can only get by booking online.

- **Beware of special rates:** A "special" rate is not necessarily the lowest rate. So, when you call, don't ask for specials, ask specifically for the lowest price and then see if you qualify for it.

- **Membership has rewards:** Sign up for membership with discount travel sites like Expedia, Hotels.com, and Booking.com. These sites have "members only" pricing that can save you cash.

- **Search engines:** All travel websites are not created equal. Some of them don't even collect the best information. Savvy consumers tout Expedia, Hotels.com, and Booking.com as some of the best, but do your own research. It pays to book travel as far in advance as possible. Waiting until the last minute could wind up costing you considerably more.

- **Book longer stays:** Staying a week instead of five or six days could yield a lower room rate.

- **New hotels want your business:** Stay at recently opened hotels, which usually offer rock bottom rates and perks to get people in the door.

- **Tipping:** Factor tips into your travel budget. While not required it's a big part of a hotel worker's income, so tip when warranted. If you're going to tip housekeeping, do it daily rather than a lump sum at the end of your stay. That way, you know it will be distributed fairly to everyone who cleaned your room. Generally, you should give the bellhop a dollar or two per bag. Many hotels include the tip for room service, but if not, tip room service the same you would a restaurant, about 15% to 20% of the bill.

- **There *is* such a thing as a free breakfast:** Check to see if the room rate includes a continental breakfast or buffet; ask if there is a way to make your morning meal part of the deal if the hotel doesn't mention it. And don't forget to check if the room has a coffee maker, if not you may want to bring along a Melita filter, coffee, and a mug. I always start my morning with a strong cup of tea topped with thick, frothy almond milk. I have my favorite mugs that I sit, sip, and start my day with. So, I always travel with my tea kit. I bring my tea, mug, and a travel size frother. If the listing you're booking doesn't mention a coffee maker, call ahead to make sure. Some hotels will bring an electric tea pot to your room so you can make your own tea or instant coffee. When I was staying in New York, for a small fee, the hotel installed a portable refrigerator so I could store my own food. It was great for my wallet and my waistline.

- **Avoid add-ons:** Make sure you factor in hotel add-on costs. Find out what they charge for parking your car, Internet, and phone calls. Consider these costs when comparing hotel pricing before your trip.

- **Hotel loyalty programs:** You will earn points to receive free rooms or upgrades. If you are good with managing your credit cards, consider using one that allows the points to go towards hotel stays.

- **Free rides:** Always see if the hotel offers a shuttle or car service. This could save you a lot of money on cabs and the savings should be factored into your cost comparisons while deciding what hotel to book.

- **More space:** Request a corner hotel room to potentially get more space for the same price.

Airbnb and Other Sharing Services

The world of vacation stays is changing radically with the advent of home sharing services like Airbnb and VRBO. The savings can be exceptional, and the experience can be unique and authentic when you are "living like a local" as Airbnb likes to say. Here are some things to keep in mind when booking a home-share.

- **Read reviews:** Home sharing sites offer reviews by past guests. Avoid locations that have few reviews. Take the reviews seriously. Hosts who have hundreds of good reviews inspire more confidence than those with a mixed bag. Airbnb has a "Superhost" designation for the top hosts on the platform. These hosts retain a high-quality level day in and day out. Be especially careful of hosts whose review section contains the reviews, "This booking was canceled days before booking." That message indicates that your booking might not be as solid as you need it to be.

- **Location, location, location:** If you need public transportation, make sure the property is close to stations and stops. If you want to walk to a coffee shop every morning, make sure one is available. You should also consider traffic conditions in the location you're staying. In high-traffic areas a property might technically be in the vicinity of the city you're visiting, but getting to attractions might mean spending long hours in the car. You can do a Google search of the area where you are booking, even before you know the actual address of the property.

- **Style:** Consider your style and look at the pictures of the dwelling. Are you OK with sharing restrooms and kitchens? If you are, Airbnb has thousands of low-priced opportunities for you all over the world. If you prefer a private apartment, that's available as well. If you are a minimalist you might not be happy staying in a vintage apartment crowded with knick-knacks, heavy curtains, and rugs.

- **Cancellation policies:** Airbnb hosts have a variety of cancelation policies, ranging from flexible to strict. If you book a room with a flexible policy, you can cancel it up to the time of check-in. A moderate cancellation policy makes it mandatory to cancel within five days of your stay or risk losing a portion of your payment. The booking fees that Airbnb charges are never refundable, unless there is a natural disaster. Read all cancellation policies very carefully; policies and procedures are subject to change.

- **Be aware of scams**: While the vast majority of Airbnb stays go off without a hitch, there have been problems with hosts listing accommodations that are not up to the quality advertised. You can always make an inquiry about the property before booking. If the host doesn't communicate with you promptly it could be a sign that you want to move on to another listing.

Staycations and Close-to-Home Vacations

Growing up, all of our family vacations were staycations or local budget vacations. We never took an airplane or a train. Instead, we would all hop in the blue station wagon, homemade sandwiches in hand, and hit the road. We usually stayed at a family friend's summer home. But one year when I was about 9, we stayed in a motel. Of course, I had to share a bed with my sisters, but I thought we were living the high life that summer. I have the best memories of all of us piling into our station wagon to take the drive up to Russian River. It was only an hour from our home, but it felt like we were a million miles away. Vacations like this are a fantastic way to have a fun break without the expense and stress of traveling. It works well for a romantic weekend getaway or a multi-family vacation.

The first step is to research cities and towns close to home. Contact their visitor's bureau to find out what attractions, discounts, and lodging deals they offer. Try to find a place to stay that has a kitchenette so that you can grocery shop and prepare most of your meals instead of eating out.

Check the Family Fun Chapter for more ideas of activities while on a staycation.

Gassing Up

The biggest expense to any road trip is the gas. People often say the best prices at the pump occur midweek. The logic generally being that business is slow on weekdays and prices go up when people hit the roads for the weekend, but you may want to rethink that strategy. A four-year analysis of gas prices by GasBuddy, a price comparison website, found this is no longer the case. Sixty-five percent of states had lower prices on the weekend and very few states had the best deals on Tuesdays and Wednesdays. The bottom-line is to do your own local research. Here are some better ways to save on gas.

- **Comparison shop:** Use gas comparison sites like GasBuddy.com. Enter your zip code and these sites will compare gas prices around town. A search I did showed that I was able to save 32¢ a gallon by driving an extra .2 of a mile instead of going on automatic pilot to my usual station. If you fill up a 16-gallon tank once a week, that's an annual savings of $266.24.

- **Pay cash:** Many stations will give you a discount (often 5¢ per gallon) when you pay with cash. Which calculates to an additional savings of $41.60 a year for that 16-gallon tank.

- **Luggage inside:** Increase fuel efficiency by keeping luggage inside the car when driving, a loaded roof rack can decrease efficiency by 5%.

- **Pack light:** An extra 100 pounds in the trunk can reduce fuel economy by 2%.

- **Use the cruise:** Cruise control maintains a constant speed on the highway; rapid acceleration and braking use more gas.

- **Tire pressure:** Check tire pressure before your trip, under-inflated tires waste fuel and are unsafe.

- **Octane**: Check your owner's manual for the most inexpensive octane gas you can use.

- **Lower the AC:** Turn down the AC, your air conditioner is a gas-guzzler. Driving with the windows down causes drag, which also uses gas. The higher the speed, the more drag. For the most fuel efficiency, roll down the windows and turn off the AC when you're cruising around town, but when you're on freeways it's windows up, AC on.

Rental Cars

Whether it's for family fun, personal use, or business travel, car rentals are one of those expenses that sneak up on you. You think it's going to be 20 bucks a day only to drop it off and the cost has doubled with add-on expenses. These tips will help you navigate the best deal when renting a car.

- **Saturday night equals savings:** Rent for a Saturday night. Monday through Friday business travel accounts for the largest chunk of car rentals. So, if your period of travel includes a Saturday night, you may qualify for lower weekend, leisure rates.

- **Five is the magic number:** Most rental companies start offering the weekly discount rate when you rent for a minimum of five days. It may be worth it to rent the car for longer than you need just to qualify for this discount.

- **Think outside the airport:** You may find better rates renting outside of the airport where you are also paying for convenience. If your hotel has a free shuttle take it into the city and rent from a downtown location. Rental prices can also vary significantly between nearby airports, so factor the cost of renting a car into airfare comparisons.

- **Use search engines:** Search for inexpensive car rentals for significant savings. Sites like CarRentals.com, Priceline, and Kayak.com give you the opportunity to compare prices from many different rental car companies at once, which is always something you should do before booking a car. Don't overlook off-brand rental agencies, which are not available everywhere, but they tend to offer anywhere from a 10% to 50% discount off what you would pay with traditional rental companies.

- **Book early:** The earlier you book your car, the better the discounts.

- **Avoid one-way rentals:** While most companies let you return a car to any of their locations, you may pay a steep price for doing so.

- **Fill the tank yourself:** Rental companies charge astronomical fuel surcharges, two to three times the rates at local gas stations. Fill the car up yourself and hold onto your receipt, some renters require proof of purchase.

- **Double your deals:** See if you can combine a coupon code discount with a membership discount from AAA or a warehouse club like Costco or BJ's.

- **Use a credit card:** Many credit cards offer built-in car rental insurance. Debit cards don't offer this service. Also, keep in mind, if you use a debit card, they may do a credit check on you and/or place a hold on funds in your bank account.

- **Rental insurance:** You may already be covered by your auto policy or even your credit card. But double check what exactly is covered. For example, some policies don't cover loss-of-use fees, which are charged each day the rental agency can't use the car because it is in the repair shop.

- **Mileage reward programs:** Check your airline mileage reward programs for deals on car rentals. Certain airlines have agreements with car rental agencies to offer better prices to their members.

- **Coupons and codes:** Before you pay cash for your rental car, search for coupons and codes to apply at check-out. Even if you already have discounts or a frequent flyer program, you can likely combine codes to double down on your savings. Sometimes you can save up to 50% off if you find the right code or coupon.

- **Pre-pay:** Many car rental companies offer two different rates: one for prepaying customers and a higher one for customers who wish to pay when they pick up the car. These savings can really add up. But keep in mind, some pre-paid offers could be non-refundable.

- **Bundle deals:** Consider including a car with your hotel or flight pricing.

- **Do you really need a car?** Finally, think about whether you really need a car every day of your trip. You might be able to get by with a few rideshares or public transportation instead of spending hundreds of dollars on a vehicle.

All-Inclusive Vacations

There are definite perks to all-inclusive vacations. We took a family trip one year and I must say it was quite easy because so much was already taken care of including activities for the kids. The key is to do your research and know exactly what is included in the all-inclusive.

- **Buy flights separately:** You may be tempted by a resort package that includes airfare, but what price are you really paying? Often, you'll have long or multiple layovers, very early flights, and the price may not even be that good. Do your homework and you can probably find a better deal booking your own airfare.

- **Watch out for add-ons:** It's never truly all-inclusive and those extras add up. Alcohol and even soda can cost you, so set a beverage budget before the trip and stick to it. Some resorts only charge for top-shelf liquor, so ask which brands are included with your package. Spas, casinos, and guided tours are just a few ways you can wind up spending extra cash at all-inclusive resorts.

- **Tipping:** Many places automatically bill you $10 to $20 per person per day extra at the end of your trip. For a family of four on a 7-day vacation that could be as much as $560 in tips. Some packages include tipping as an added promotional extra. It's worth asking about when booking your stay.

- **Choose the right resort:** What kind of vacation setting do you want? A serene setting? Great parties? Activities for the kids? Don't stop at price and policies, research a resort's reputation and atmosphere, too. For example, there are adult-only resorts like Sandals, which are perfect for a romantic getaway or a girls' trip, and then there are family-friendly destinations like Club Med or Disney Cruises. It's easy to do this research by reading reviews on websites like TripAdvisor, as well as the resort's own website.

- **Make it a group:** Groups are typically made up of 10 travelers, but some companies will give group discounts and perks to groups of eight. Just ask. The rates are usually lower for groups.

- **Buy ahead:** Buy excursions ahead of time. Many tour operators allow you to pre-book excursions, so you can save and have less to worry about once you are on your trip. Some travel agents sweeten the pot when signing up for cruises and resorts by offering extra coupons and bonuses that can be used on excursions.

- **Consider the interior:** If you don't need fancy accommodations, then you can save big bucks booking a small interior room on a cruise ship. Ask at check-in whether there is an upgrade available for free.

- **Coupons, loyalty programs, rewards:** Before you sign on the dotted line, search for coupons and sign up for loyalty and reward programs. By now you know these techniques can yield big results.

- **What's the weather?** June through November is hurricane season, so resorts and cruises offer some very low rates to the Caribbean and Mexico then. January through March is known as Wave Season in the cruise industry and you may be able to find extra incentives like lower fares or on-board credits. If you enjoy multiple vacations a year, these deals might be right for you. Just make sure you are protected. Most resorts have a hurricane protection policy, plus you can purchase travel insurance and still spend less than you would if you traveled during peak season. But before buying insurance, check with your credit card company to see whether you're covered when you charge travel expenses. Also, keep in mind a resort's hurricane protection policy usually means they will give you a travel voucher, not a refund. That doesn't do you much good unless you plan another tropical vacation and chances are, you'll still have to pay for the airfare, which could mean out-of-pocket costs to you.

Last-Minute Travel

Last-minute travel is a gamble. You may find the deal of a lifetime or end up paying big bucks.

- **Airfares:** The biggest pitfall of last-minute travel can be airfare costs. If you can't find a flight within your budget, check vacation packages. Agencies buy bulk plane tickets in advance, then bundle them with hotels and car rentals. As the trip dates approach, agencies need to sell these packages or it will be a loss to them.

- **Shop midweek**: Look midweek for web only deals you can use that weekend.

- **Travel auctions:** Check out travel auction sites. Priceline's "Inside Track" gives you a lot of data on fares and trends so you can bid accordingly.

- **Fly standby:** Flying standby is an economical option if you have flexibility, but it's not a good idea if you're traveling in a group or need to check luggage.

- **Last-minute cruises:** If you want to take a cruise, you may actually benefit from last-minute travel. Travelers usually have 60 to 90 days before departure to cancel and get a full refund. After that, ships have a good estimate of capacity and they start to slash prices. Search for websites devoted to finding the least-expensive, last-minute cruise prices.

Travel by Train

If your destination isn't too far, consider taking a bus or train, which can be inexpensive and include amenities like free wi-fi. If you are traveling with kids, you may be able to find deep discounts. I have found as much as 50% off train tickets for kids under the age of 16.

- **Buy ahead**: Don't purchase your ticket the day of travel, save money with an advance ticket. Sometimes you can get this discount even if you're booking the night before departure.

- **Attraction discounts:** Sometimes you can find destination discounts at local museums or restaurants for train riders who show their ticket.

- **Refunds and discounts:** Some trains will give you a full or partial refund if your train is delayed or arrives late.

- **Sleeping on board:** If it's a longer trip, book a sleeping car or a couchette. This will save you money on stopping overnight at a motel not to mention saving your back by trying to sleep in a regular seat. Before booking a train, ask if meals, towels, and linens will be included with your fare.

Traveling with a Wheelchair

If you are traveling with a wheelchair make sure you take as many precautions as possible to ensure your chair arrives in the condition it was in when you boarded the flight.

One story that I worked on for both *USA Today* and CBS 5 really demonstrated the frustrations of people traveling by plane with a wheelchair. Many of these passengers arrive to their destination with their wheelchairs broken in pieces. As one person I interviewed said, "It's like arriving with both of your legs broken." Here are some tips for avoiding this serious problem.

- **Before you travel:** Check with the manufacturer to see what parts may be removable to take on the plane with you. Leave a large note with specific instructions taped to the chair so employees can follow loading instructions. Securely wrap any parts that are attached to the chair.

- **File a claim:** If your wheelchair is damaged, immediately file a claim.

- **Find a rental shop:** Some experts recommend checking in advance to see if the area you are traveling to has a wheelchair rental shop with your model in stock should you need to rent a wheelchair.

When I finished the investigation into how some airlines treat wheelchairs, I received an email from a viewer that brought me to tears.

"Ms. Pavini, THANK YOU! The helplessness, rage, fear & ineptitude I felt as I was presented with my destroyed transportation...... My legs..... it was indescribable. It could only have been dropped from a significant height (I've tipped-over in my chair, missed doorways at 5+ mph and never done more than scuff it... They destroyed it, even shearing solid steel bolts!) Then, to add insult to injury, the cavalier attitude, the expectation that I can just wait for them &/or "make due" with inferior/painful/dangerous "temporary replacement equipment". The months.... Ok I'm going to stop. You cannot know how much it means that you have chosen to give one of us a voice, you just can't. Again, THANK YOU!" - Robert

It's emails like these that give me the energy to continue the good fight for consumer protections!

Other Travel Tidbits

- **Big tourist destinations:** If you have your heart set on visiting a popular travel destination, make sure you book tickets well in advance. Waiting until the last minute could break the bank or your heart.

- **Multi-generational travel**: If you are planning a trip for the whole extended family, getting it on everyone's calendar ahead of time usually results in lower prices. Because popular attractions often sell out during peak seasons, booking early ups the odds of finding tickets to the activities everyone has their hearts set on.

- **School breaks**: Thanksgiving, Christmas, and Spring Break school holidays are usually busy. Book flights and hotels to popular tourist attractions as far in advance as you can for these busy seasons or risk paying top dollar.

- **Complicated trips**: Safaris and cruises to places like Antarctica require complicated itineraries booked through multiple agencies. Some require vaccinations. These types of vacations require planning not only for the best prices, but also for your health and safety.

- **Using miles**: If you have your heart set on a luxury vacation using miles, it can sometimes take up to two years to find dates where you will cash in your miles.

Credit Cards

Most American credit cards charge foreign transaction fees when used abroad and these fees can add up. International credit cards have no transaction fees and can be used all over the world. These cards often have better rates on currency conversion, too. The very best international cards have great rewards programs, travel insurance, and other perks. Some of these cards carry an annual fee, but some are free. Whether you have an international card or not, make sure you check with your credit card company to let them know you will be traveling out of the country. Some cards automatically block foreign transactions to avoid fraud when charges are made far from home. Also check for fees associated with ATM withdrawals while traveling abroad.

Cell Phones

If you use your American cell phone in another country you will find yourself with a very hefty bill when you get home, if you don't make arrangements before you leave. This is a must. You also may find that your cell phone doesn't even work in some foreign countries. Since every cell service provider has different plans, you'll have to check with your carrier and see what your best option is. If you are on a short trip, you may be able to add international calling to your phone on a per-day basis. You also may be able to buy a monthly plan that covers international calls for a reasonable fee. Unfortunately, mistakes can still happen, so get everything in writing and a confirmation number when you add these services. A friend was recently in Canada and arranged for a Canadian plan before she left. The phone company woke her in the middle of the night to ask if she realized her current phone bill was $1,000. Luckily, she had her confirmation code handy. In addition to cell phone plans, some other options include:

- Apps like Skype or WhatsApp for Internet voice and texting

- Buy an inexpensive unlocked phone at your destination

- Buy a SIM card for your unlocked phone

- Use your tablet for Internet voice and texting

Be realistic about your need to communicate via phone. Some of us can do all the communicating we need to do online. And if by chance your phone is lost or stolen, contact your carrier immediately.

Helping Others

If you're lucky enough to amass airline miles, you may be able to donate them to a non-profit like the Make A Wish Foundation or the American Red Cross. Just check with your airline's frequent flier program to see how.

Travel Resources

Legal Rights: www.travellaw.com

For Travel Advice, Advisories, and to Report Problems or Complaints: Department of Transportation

To Save When Driving: GasBuddy.com, AAA Fuel Cost Calculator

13. HELP WITH HEALTHCARE COSTS

One thing that my father could count on was medical insurance for our family through his job. When I was growing up, we didn't think about insurance, it just came along with the job. And in those days, medical insurance was less confusing. You didn't need an expert to explain which plan was best for your specific needs.

Over my 20- plus years of reporting, questions about medical care and coverage have topped the list of consumer concerns. And understandably so. Uncovered medical expenses are among the top reasons for financial stress and bankruptcy in this country. Deciphering medical plans is next to impossible without some guidance. I recall a news story I did on a family that didn't have full medical coverage. Their young son accidentally injured his eye. The costs for the emergency room visit and sight-saving procedures were about $28,000. If they'd had the right insurance coverage, the bill would have been a third of what they were required to pay. After the story aired, my phone wouldn't stop ringing. So many viewers had similar stories to report. I wish there was an easy answer to questions raised about medical insurance and the healthcare system. Policies do change and depending on where you live, the rules may vary. Here are some insights and resources that could help simplify some of your future healthcare cost questions.

The Rising Cost of Healthcare Today

There's nothing healthy about American healthcare costs. The price we pay for everything health-related continues to rise at a significant rate, year after year.

A 2016 Kaiser Family Foundation Survey reports that more than 25% of U.S. adults struggle to keep up with their medical bills, even if they have insurance. The problem is so serious that medical debt is now the No. 1 cause of personal bankruptcy filings in the U.S.

The cost of healthcare is outstripping people's ability to pay the bills, but price isn't the only problem. It's notoriously difficult, if not impossible, to comparison shop for medical treatments and procedures. To make decisions even more difficult, research by the Department of Health and Human Services shows that when it comes to healthcare, there is often no correlation between quality and price, so consumers can be paying top dollar for low-quality care by providers and hospitals. The complexity of insurance plans and billing protocols can spell financial disaster for uninformed consumers. In this chapter, I'll point out some of the common blind spots that can cost you, and some ways you can save hundreds of dollars a year.

One resource that is too good not to mention right off the bat is Fairhealthconsumer.org. Their mission is to help you understand your healthcare costs and coverage, and to bring transparency to pricing and insurance. Health insurance companies around the country send them more than a billion medical claims a year. The organization uses information from those bills to estimate what providers charge, and what insurance companies and consumers typically pay for services. Consumers can find this information and other money saving articles and tips by logging onto their site.

The Right Coverage

Medical coverage is one place where it not only pays to do your homework, it's dangerous not to. Even if you get coverage through your employer, reading your policy closely, and understanding what's covered, pays off. Let's start with the positive aspects of understanding your plan. Most insurance plans offer a variety of wellness and preventative benefits. Check your plan for these popular but often overlooked perks.

- gym memberships

- meditation and yoga classes

- nutrition and diet resources

- tobacco cessation programs

- wellness coaching

- preventative treatments like breast cancer screenings and teeth cleanings

Wellness Classes

Many hospitals offer free wellness classes. For example, our local hospital recently offered a nutrition class for people with pre-diabetes and diabetes. The classes range from healthy eating to preventing disease. I think these programs offer a wealth of information to keep you healthy. You can check online to find out what is coming up and also find out if any classes are offered virtually.

On the Downside

The side effects of not understanding your plan can also be dangerous to your financial health. Not only are you potentially missing out on benefits, but maybe even paying for things already covered. The penalty for using care that is not covered or is out-of-network can cost thousands of dollars. Luckily, there is help available to support you in choosing the best plan. Here are some things to keep in mind.

Low-price premiums can cost you. When it comes to choosing a plan, whether you have employer-sponsored care or not, it's important to look beyond the price tag. A plan that has a $200 a month premium cost, but a $10,000 out-of-pocket deductible, may not be a better deal than a plan with a $500 monthly premium and a $4,000 deductible. In addition to deductibles, there are variable co-payments and prescription prices to think about. Your choice depends on how you use the healthcare system. Consider how often you visit the doctor, if you have any ongoing or chronic medical conditions, prescription medications, and any other factors. It's not unusual for people to need assistance when it comes to choosing the best insurance plan.

Finding Help Understanding Your Plan

• **Human resources**: You can ask your human resources department for help understanding your plan options. While HR might not be able to give you in-depth information on each and every plan, they should be able to help you understand the pros and cons of the different company offerings.

• **Websites**: Sites like Fairhealthconsumer.org might provide the support you need. As we mentioned above, Fair Health Consumer analyzes actual consumer bills for a variety of services in various locations around the country. They help you understand the going rate for procedures and help you compare value of medical institutions. You can use this information to make sure the doctors in the plan you choose are practicing at the best value hospitals and health networks in your area.

- **Healthcare navigators**: Navigators are trained and able to help consumers, small businesses, and their employees as they look for health coverage options through their state's health insurance marketplace. They not only help people find plans, they can help with completing eligibility and enrollment forms. Navigators are required to be unbiased. They understand how to access information tailored to your personal needs. Their services are free to consumers. Check out Healthcare.gov to get started.

I hope with these resources, you'll be able to access a plan that's best for you and your family.

National Health Awareness Months

Many health-related advocacy groups have an entire month dedicated to bringing awareness and understanding to various chronic diseases. For example, October is Breast Cancer Awareness Month, November is Crohn's and Colitis Awareness Month, and February is American Heart Month. During these months, many organizations offer free screenings, classes and resources.

Health Savings Accounts

A Health Savings Account (HSA) is like a tax-free, personal savings account, but it can only be used for qualified healthcare expenses. To be eligible, you must be enrolled in a high-deductible health plan (HDHP). Before you decide an HSA is the answer to your high-cost insurance premiums, it's important to weigh the advantages and disadvantages, which will be different for every person. If you're generally healthy and want to save for future planned healthcare expenses, an HSA may be a good choice. Likewise, if you're near retirement, an HSA may make sense because the money can be used to offset the costs of medical care after retirement. Your HSA dollars typically can be used to help pay the health insurance deductible and other qualified medical expenses. Dental care, vision care, prescription glasses, and incidentals are expenses that add up and are usually covered. Any funds you withdraw for non-qualified medical expenses will be taxed at your income tax rate, plus a 10% tax penalty. Having a high-deductible plan means you are going to pay more money out of pocket before your medical coverage kicks in. Your upfront costs will be higher whenever you have to use your medical coverage during the year until the deductible is reached. Unspent money in an HSA rolls over at the end of the year so it's available for future health expenses.

High-deductible health plans, which are a requirement for HSAs, aren't always the best option, especially if you expect to have significant healthcare expenses in the future. You may be better off with an insurance plan that charges higher premiums upfront but covers a greater percentage of costs.

Comparison Shopping Resources

When a treatment or procedure is not an emergency, you might be able to do some planning to estimate and potentially limit the costs. Here are some resources to help you prepare for major events like the birth of a child or non-urgent surgery. You can also find out which hospitals in your area provide the best quality service and which physicians practice at the hospital.

- **FAIR Health Consumer:** As we mentioned earlier, this organization is a font of valuable consumer information on medical pricing and quality.

- **Healthcare Bluebook**: This non-profit's mission is to help protect consumers from low-quality, high-cost healthcare. They help consumers save money on out-of-pocket expenses. The Healthcare Bluebook app is especially helpful for saving money on tests like CT scans and MRIs. Not only does it compare pricing, it compares quality of the providers so you can understand whether you're getting a good deal or not.

- **Guroo.com:** Guroo is the consumer arm of the non-profit Health Care Cost Institute. You'll find data on healthcare costs and quality with national, state, and local prices.

- **Medicare**: Medicare pricing is available to the public through their website, you can use it for cost comparison.

Training Programs
Save on Dental, Optical, and Mental Health

This can be a gamechanger. Dental, optical, and mental health school training programs all need patients for students to work with. These students are supervised by some of the finest professionals in their field. The cost for treatment at these facilities is often far lower than you would pay at a regular office. For instance, at our local community college dental training clinic, cleanings may cost about $10 for children and $25 for adults after a one-time $5 evaluation. (The $5 is waived for students and staff at the college.) This is compared to the typical price range for a regular cleaning is usually between $70 and $200 without X-rays. While the price is definitely a bargain, you'll typically have to spend more time at the office or clinic. To find providers with student practitioners, search in your area for medical schools, dental schools, optometry programs, and student therapists (for mental health). You can also check out the website of your local college or university for information. I did several stories on these programs and was quite impressed by not only the practitioners but the vast range of services and procedures offered. Many of these schools will also work with patients on a sliding scale based on their income.

Take the Pain Out of Prescription Prices

Like other healthcare costs, the price of prescription drugs is going up consistently. In 2020 alone, the cost of more than 560 medications shot up, according to GoodRx, a company that tracks prescription drug prices and helps consumers find discounts.

It's important to keep in mind that it's not uncommon for physicians to be unaware of the cost consumers pay for the drugs they prescribe. A friend was shocked when the pharmacist told her the asthma prescription was going to be $165. She told him not to fill it, and called her doctor, who was flabbergasted. The doctor found another medicine that cost less than $30. It's OK to let your doctor know that you need the lowest possible cost for your prescriptions. You can also ask your pharmacist if there is a lower-cost alternative when having the prescription filled.

Here are some tried and true methods to save some money on drugs.

- **GoodRx:** GoodRx is an invaluable resource for information on drug prices and more. The organization gathers prices from tens of thousands of pharmacies across the U.S. in a database offering up-to-date information about what drugs cost and how you can save. And GoodRx will send you a drug savings card that can be used for discounts of up to 80% on most prescription drugs at virtually every U.S. pharmacy.

- **Generics:** Generic drugs have the same active ingredients as brand-name medications, but generics are substantially less expensive. For example, one major cholesterol-lowering drug on the market retails for about $390 for a 30-day supply. The generic version is about $10 for a 30-day supply. Always ask your doctor if a generic is available. If there is no generic available, ask if there's a similar drug that does have a generic. You can also get very low prices on generics by shopping at big box retailers. Stores like Target, Walmart, and some larger grocery stores have lists of generic drugs that cost $4 for a 30-day supply and $10 for a 90-day supply. Costco may have generics for even less. Many pharmacies in grocery stores and big-box chains also offer the same pricing. Ask for the list when you're at the pharmacy or look it up on the Internet and bring a copy to your doctor. Different chains have different lists; you can usually find the lists online. These prices are sometimes so low, that your cost might be cheaper if you buy them *without* insurance than to pay the co-pay with your insurance.

One of the most eye-opening consumer stories I did was on not only how much you could save by using generics, but how much you could save depending on where you bought the generics. I followed a woman who had to take four prescription medications. We compared the four generic versions at four different pharmacies. The costs were drastically different. The most expensive total for the four medications was about $137, and the lowest was about $13 at Costco. It can be as easy as making a phone call to all the pharmacies and warehouse clubs in your area to compare costs. In most states you do not need a club membership to utilize warehouse club pharmacies.

- **Coupons:** There are coupons for almost everything, and prescription drugs are no exception. Some noted companies offering coupons include GoodRx, Single Care and Needy

Meds. These are just a few of the companies that offer coupons for many common medications. Pharmacies and drug manufacturers also offer coupons. Search online for more.

- **Free samples:** Ask your doctor if there are free samples available.

- **Loyalty programs:** The loyalty card from your pharmacy can help reduce your drug costs. Drugstore deals at the three biggest pharmacy chains in the U.S. — CVS, Rite Aid, and Walgreens — work like this: You sign up free of charge and earn points by using pharmacy services; things like filling prescriptions, getting a vaccine, or checking your blood glucose levels. Those points translate into discounts, sometimes hefty ones, or reward dollars you can spend in the store. Don't forget that over-the-counter medications often go on sale, and you can get an additional discount using your loyalty card. Combining that sale price and loyalty card with a coupon can dramatically lower the cost of over-the-counter medications. Often the highest value coupons are for over-the-counter medications.

- **Bigger bottles:** Instead of getting a prescription that lasts for 30 days, and making an insurance copay each time, ask if your insurance will allow a 90-day supply so you can make just one copay every three months. Discounts for generics at big box stores are also greater on 90-day supplies. This works for medications you take long-term.

- **Patient assistance programs:** Patient assistance programs (PAPs) are usually sponsored by pharmaceutical companies as a "safety net" for Americans who have no health insurance or are underinsured. The goal of these programs is to provide financial assistance to help these patients access drugs for little or no cost. Nonprofit organizations that help you find assistance include: Needy Meds and Partnership for Prescription Assistance. Other resources include state assistance programs and Medicare Extra Help. You can also call the manufacturer of your medication directly.

Saving on Supplements

Many of the same strategies for saving on prescription medications work for supplements, too. Generics, big bottles, pill splitting, coupons, and loyalty programs all exist for supplements, just like they do for prescriptions. If your daily routine includes supplements, here are some additional better ways to save.

- **Multivitamins:** Check labels and see if you can find the combinations you need in one pill.

- **Prescription supplements:** Ask your doctor if there is a prescription available for your supplement. It might be part of a big box store generic formulary, meaning you may be able to get the prescription filled for $4, or less.

Mental Health Resources

Unfortunately, mental health resources may be one of the first things to be cut when budgets are adjusted. Mental health is as important as our physical health and often is ignored. Take advantage of free or low-cost resources available to you.

- Resources from The Substance Abuse and Mental Health Services Administration, SAMHSA, offers 24/7 referrals and information.

- The National Institute of Mental Health (NIMH.NIH.GOV) is another place to find resources for those suffering from a range of mental health issues.

- The Anxiety and Depression Association of America, ADAA, helps people find support.

- Suicide Prevention is a phone call away for anyone who needs to talk. Currently the number is: 1-800-273-8255

Medical Billing Errors

Medical billing errors are not uncommon, and when they happen, the financial toll can be grave. While there are no comprehensive statistics on medical-billing mistakes, groups that review bills on patients' behalf report that more than 75% of bills contain errors.

The medical billing process is complicated and confusing, it can be difficult for consumers to learn the cost of treatments before they are administered. While you wouldn't buy a car without understanding the price before you drive off the lot, it has been impossible for consumers to estimate what the total cost of a medical procedure will be ahead of time. This means more legwork for you. You'll need to ask a lot of questions both before and after you receive treatment, and you'll have to be the one to bring up the topic, as many medical providers won't.

214

There has been a push for medical bill transparency in billing practices on state and national levels. Some states already require transparency, and national laws are set to go into effect in 2021. The laws make it easier to find the information, but consumers will still need to do the footwork.

Decoding Your Medical Bills

Very few of us can decipher a medical bill without becoming dazed and confused. You won't be alone if you suspect the codes and abbreviations are a foreign language. The industry standard of bundling charges together without itemizing individual charges can muddy the water even more.

It's very important to ask the doctor and hospital for itemized bills, and to check them over carefully. If you suspect errors, you can start by reporting them to the physician or institution doing the billing. Many people find it's difficult to connect with insurance companies when it comes to correcting errors. The problem is so common that a whole industry of healthcare advocates has sprung up to meet the needs of consumers.

Healthcare advocates are devoted to helping patients who are overcharged or who are unable to pay their medical bills. If you don't get satisfaction on your own, it might be in your interest to engage a healthcare advocate to fight your case for you. Advocates typically charge 25% of the money they recover for you.

Buyer Beware

I have done several stories on people who try to save money on non- covered medical procedures and surgeries such as plastic surgery by going to other countries or cut-rate doctors. This is no bargain and can end up costing you your health and even your life. The same goes for certain medi-spa treatments. These are procedures that are done in spas overseen by a medical doctor. The story I worked on showed that the doctor was not onsite to oversee the actual treatments as he was responsible for several medi-spas at the same time. The woman I interviewed went in for a laser hair removal procedure on her legs. Her skin was brown but when she left, she had white spots covering both of her legs. She was devastated because there was nothing she could do to reverse the new permanent de-pigmentation.

The American Society for Dermatologic Surgery Association suggests these safety tips for medi-spas.

• **Physician available:** Make sure a doctor is on site.

• **Ask questions:** How many times has your aesthetician performed the procedure.

• **Test first:** Ask for a test patch if you're uncertain about a particular procedure or have sensitive skin, as it's easier to treat a complication on a small area of skin.

• **Don't ignore pain:** Contact the spa's medical director or your own doctor immediately if you experience pain, discomfort, or discoloration. If you don't get a response and are concerned, consider going to the ER.

- **Better Business Bureau:** Research medical spas by contacting the local Better Business Bureau. Ask the spa for referrals and check the on-site doctor's credentials.

Hospice and Palliative Care

I waited too long to connect with hospice when my father was nearing the end of his battle with cancer. For many people, there is a feeling of giving up or admitting a loved one is dying that keeps us from setting up hospice care. But nothing could be further from the truth. Hospice helps families in ways you might not even think you need. Hospice addresses the physical, emotional, and spiritual needs of the patient. They offer 24/7 support for the family and caregivers. I had a question about my father's breathing at 2 a.m. and the kindest and most knowledgeable person was on the other end of the phone when I called. She walked me through what I needed to do and was reassuring. They will arrange for hospital beds, different types of home healthcare needs, showers, counseling, and dozens of other things to help patients and families during this time. In fact, in many ways they can prolong someone's life while making it more comfortable. I was so impressed by hospice that I did two stories on them. As I did my research for the stories, I found that hospice also offers palliative care, specialized care for people living with a serious illness. This means that someone can still be receiving treatments while receiving hospice services.

Professionally and personally, I highly recommend what hospice offers. Hospicesect.org is a good place to find out what is available for you.

Caregiver Resources

When we were caring for my mom during a serious illness, our local hospital offered a caregiver support group. I went with my father and it was really helpful. We only went once, but we picked up on some really good resources that eventually helped us. Most hospitals offer these types of classes, resources, and meetings. When you are overseeing the care of a family member or friend, it is imperative to get support and help for yourself. It's only a phone call or online search to find out what is available in your area.

Helping Others

If you have a background in healthcare you may be able to volunteer for non-profit clinics. This goes for mental healthcare clinics and programs as well. Hospice has training programs for volunteers to work with families. Suicide prevention also trains volunteers and can be a very rewarding way to give back.

14. WHAT TO BUY WHEN

Hidden in a neighborhood of San Francisco was a bakery outlet where my mom and I would go every few weeks to stock up on baked goods. Often the deals were so great, mom would buy extra loaves to freeze. As we scoured the shelves for bargains, I would find my way to my favorite rack: the fruit pies. They were 10 cents and I got to pick the flavors.

The bread and pies were nearly as good as when they came out of the oven. There was no shame in going into an outlet or "day-old" bakery. My parents taught me that if you can get a deal on something, why wouldn't you? That mindset has stayed with me my entire life and serves me well to this day.

I took this love of a good deal to work with me. When I was working at CBS 5 in San Francisco, I had a regular Friday segment called, "Best of Bay Area Bargains." In my three minutes, I would highlight great deals that would be happening that weekend throughout the Bay Area. The response was overwhelming. In fact, this one segment was the launching pad for my own show, *The Real Deal*.

One afternoon while an executive for the network was visiting our station, I was brought in to meet him. It just happened that as I walked into the office that Friday, a Best of

Bay Area Bargains segment was airing. The segment was about a store that sold everything you would need to remodel your bathroom at about 70% less than the usual retail price. After I introduced myself, I said, "See that segment airing right now. That segment will bring more traffic to our website than anything else we air today." Well, this piqued his interest. I went on to explain what these segments were about and how people really want resources to save money. I pitched him my idea for a 30-minute show based on deals. I explained that we had already put the time, money, and effort into creating these segments, so it would just take a little extra time to edit them into a program. Within five minutes I got the go ahead and *The Real Deal* was born. The show aired for many years and was the recipient of many Press Club Awards. I learned a long time ago that you can make things happen if you are prepared when an opportunity arises.

We had a fan base that was dedicated to saving money. I loved running into viewers who were excited to share about the bargains they found. It was also great to help the merchants. Once I found out about an outlet that sold candles. These candles, which were sold wholesale to high-end retail stores, had slight imperfections. When they didn't pass quality control, they were shipped to this little outlet in Burlingame, Calif. The outlet would sell these treasures twice a year for a buck or two a candle. Other items would be about 75% off. The Friday evening before the sale I aired my story. I called the store manager that Monday to see how it went. She said, "I have three words for you. 'Oh My God.' She went on to tell me when she arrived an hour before the store opened the line to get in was blocks long. And that they usually did about $1,800 at these sales, but this weekend they did about $18,000. I realized I was really onto something.

I loved doing these segments. Seeking out these hidden treasure troves and getting paid for it was a dream come true. Eventually, I took a similar concept and began writing a monthly Best Buys column for *MarketWatch* and *The Wall Street Journal Sunday*. Here I would highlight what purchases are at a low price for that particular month. Below is a compilation of this money saving calendar. There may be other times during the year that you will find deals on these items, but historically these are the best times to buy.

January

For many of us hitting the stores and shopping is the last thing on our mind in January. After weeks of holiday shopping and returning, no matter how great the deal may be, we want to steer clear of spending. But before you write off the idea of shopping, you may want to consider some of the best things to buy this month.

- **Linens:** This might be one of the oldest January Best Buys in history. In 1878, John Wanamaker, the father of department stores, introduced the first White Sale. For over 140 years, it has become a tradition for stores to offer some of their best prices on bedding, linens, and towels during the first month of the year.

- **Furniture:** Historically, this is the month when many furniture manufacturers release their new designs. This means stores need to clear out older inventory to make room for the new. If you are in the market for darker color schemes, look for closeout prices on fall and winter fabrics to save even more. Remember: if you are purchasing a large piece of furniture measure your doorways into your home and the room where you will be putting the furniture. Then measure the width of the piece you will be buying. I have heard too many horror stories of furniture arriving and the delivery people cannot get the furniture through the door.

- **Gym memberships:** It's always one of the most popular New Year's resolutions: getting in shape. And gyms depend on our enthusiasm to tackle that resolution with the purchase of a gym membership. Many clubs offer incentives in January. There are a variety of discounts you might be able to score, including waived enrollment fees, free personal training sessions, or a friends-and-family discount. Before signing up, be sure to read all the fine print. If you are in the habit of joining a gym and not going after a few months (that would be me), you don't want to be locked into a long-term agreement.

- **Winter produce:** Buy seasonal and you'll get the best price and quality. Plan menus around cruciferous veggies like broccoli, cauliflower, cabbage, kale, brussels sprouts, collards, watercress, and radishes. Root vegetables like beets and turnips are also in season. Most cruciferous veggies are rich in vitamins and minerals such as folate and vitamin K. Citrus fruits like oranges, lemons, and grapefruit are also at the market. You can cook up meals and freeze them for later use when the winter produce is on its way out.

- **Gift cards:** Many of us have been there: we get a gift card to a place we can't find anything we will really use. After Christmas, many people try to exchange gift cards they received for the ones they actually want. Look on gift card exchange websites to buy cards at a discounted rate. They can sell for up to 35% less than their face value, although around 10% appears to be the norm especially for more popular stores. Check regularly as you can find some gift cards for practical items like groceries, gas, restaurants, or office supplies. And if you are the recipient of gift cards you won't be using, consider selling them in January.

- **Calendars:** One resolution that always seems to be a theme for me is to get organized. And I would search out the perfect calendar system. I am still a pen-to-planner kind of gal. I don't use an electronic calendar for most of my planning. If you are able to stay organized until about mid-January without purchasing a calendar, you will be able to save significantly on most calendars and planners by waiting a few weeks.

- **Dress clothes:** As stores make room for spring styles, you can find deals on dressy clothing, suits, slacks, and blouses from the fall and holidays. Now would be a good time to update your work wardrobe. And I am a fan of consignment and resale shops were the deals are usually rock-bottom.

• **Carpeting and flooring:** Summer and Fall are typically the seasons when most homes are sold, which means people are changing carpeting during those months to spruce it up. Since January is a slower month for carpeting and flooring companies, this can mean a fantastic time to find deals. Don't be afraid to negotiate on pricing, delivery, and other discounts. Look for carpet remnants for deep savings. These are large pieces of carpet that are leftover or discontinued.

• **Televisions:** There is no doubt that Black Friday is typically the best time to find a deal on TVs. But what many consumers may not realize is you can usually find better deals on higher quality TVs in January as Super Bowl Sunday approaches. Here's an even better way to save, ask about open box TVs. These are returns or floor models that usually offer additional discounts. Make sure they offer the same warranty. After the holidays is a fantastic time to find these steals since there are lots of returns, which means more open box sales for you.

February

Even though February is the shortest month of the year, it certainly doesn't lack deals. Here are just a few additional reasons to love the month of heart health and Valentine's Day even more.

- **Electronics:** Historically Black Friday is about the best time to buy electronics, but don't underestimate February. CES, formerly known as the Consumer Electronics Show, which is usually held in January, highlights all of the new electronics hitting the market for the upcoming year. So, what does that mean to you? You'll find deals on the prior year models. Stores need to clear their warehouses and shelves to make room for new merchandise. Here again the open-box tip comes into play. Refurbished items are another way to save on some of the most popular brands of electronics. In both cases, make sure the item is in perfect condition and they offer the same warranty as a new item.

- **Movies:** As this book goes to press, there's uncertainty over when movie theaters and production will be back to normal. Traditionally, February is Oscar month. Cinemark's Oscar Movie Week is one if my favorite deals. I catch all of the Oscar-nominated movies with a single pass. Typically, you can purchase a movie pass sometime during the beginning of February. In 2020 the movie pass was $35 and allowed participants to watch all 10 movies. That averaged out to $3.50 per movie. Other theaters may offer promotions as well.

- **Tax software:** Right around February we start to think about April 15th and our taxes. In February, you can find deals on tax software. Be sure to search for coupon codes if you are purchasing your software programs online. The AARP Foundation Tax-Aide Program offers individualized tax preparation to people 50 and older with low- to moderate-income levels at no charge. There are more than 5,000 locations across the country. The IRS also offers the Volunteer Income Tax Assistance program (VITA) and the Tax Counseling for the Elderly program (TCE). You can find out if you qualify for these programs by going to IRS.gov.

- **Winterwear and winter gear:** February plays host to Presidents' Day Weekend, which is known for a variety of sales. You can find particularly good deals on outerwear. Here again, stores need to sell off winter clothing so there is plenty of room for Spring items. This is the time of year I always buy our coats and warm sweaters. Look for deals up to 75% off and check for store coupons to save more. Skiers will also start seeing winter sports gear such as skis and ski clothing with lower price tags.

- **Perfume and cologne:** It's rare to find department stores with cosmetics, perfume, and cologne on sale, but they do offer special promotions typically two or three times a year. Once around the holidays, Mother's Day, and Valentine's Day. Some manufacturers offer a gift with purchase, giving the consumer a bigger bang for their buck.

- **A healthy heart:** February is American Heart Month. Local hospitals and community centers will be offering complimentary or low-cost lectures and workshops to educate people on how to keep heart healthy. You can find a wealth of information at Healthfinder.gov and Heart.org.

- **Canned foods:** It's National Canned Food Month. Expect to find deals on a wide range of canned foods. If you do nothing else, make sure you are a member of your grocery store's free loyalty card program to ensure you get the deals. Look for coupons to save even more. And because canned foods have a longer shelf life, be sure to stock up.

- **Flowers:** Valentine's Day will keep the prices of roses at their peak. If you must give a bouquet on this special day, you can find less expensive flowers and plants. If your heart is set on roses, check with stores like Trader Joe's. They usually have very reasonable pricing on all of their floral bouquets, including roses. If you live near a flower market (where local florists go to buy their flowers), consider shopping there. Most flower markets have certain daily hours where they are open to the public.

March

When I think of March, I think of change. We have a change in time with Daylight Savings, a change of season as spring begins, and we tend to do our Spring cleaning: out with the old and in with the new. Luckily, some of the new items you may be looking for will be on sale during the 31 glorious days of March.

- **Spring cleaning savings:** As the first day of Spring approaches, so do the deals on spring cleaning products. Here it may pay off to purchase brand name cleaners while they are on sale. Some come with a more concentrated formula, which means you can get the job done more efficiently with less product. Bonus tip: Vinegar is a surprisingly versatile all-purpose cleaner and it tends to go on sale this month.

- **Hitting the slopes:** This month is known for blowout clearance events and parking lot sales at sporting goods stores. Some shops that rent goods will host end-of-season sales on used winter gear. They typically upgrade to new models every season. Stores with trade-in programs are also likely to sell gently used gear at discounted prices. Trade-in programs are designed for people who want the greatest and latest gear. For example, a store could give you 50% in store credit if you trade in your ski or board equipment within one year. Then you can use that store credit to buy a new board and your old board will be sold to someone looking to buy used.

- **Summer camps:** Even if you're still living in the cold of winter, don't shiver away from the deals on summer camps. Now is the time to think about camps, especially if you have more than one child and if you are looking for a discount. By booking early, you can help to ensure your child has a place in the camp of their choice and qualify for any early enrollment discounts.

- **Golf clubs:** If you are in the market for a new set of golf clubs, March is your month. For some manufacturers, their new models will be coming out soon and that means prior models are discounted. Another thought is to check out resale shops like Play it Again Sports that specialize in sporting goods. I did a story on these stores and some of the deals were pretty amazing. People often sell their used clubs to help cover the cost of their new set. What that means to resale shop customers is clubs that are in really good condition at a fraction of the full retail price.

- **Frozen foods:** March is National Frozen Food Month. Not only will you find savings at the grocery store, but a lot of manufacturers will offer special promotions and coupons. Stay in the know by following your favorite brands on social media. This way you will have access to special promotions, coupons, and offers. Combine these coupons with your grocery store rewards savings to really cash in.

- **Arts and crafts:** If you love crafting, you will love this month. March is National Craft Month, which means not only are there deals on crafting supplies, but many stores will offer a range of crafting events and classes. Check with your local craft stores to find out what programs they will be offering and if they offer any classes virtually. In the past, stores like Michaels have offered classes for kids, sometimes for as little as a couple of dollars, including the supplies.

- **Gardening supplies:** As the time to start planting approaches, the savings will grow. Expect to find deals on just about everything that has to do with gardening. Add your name to local gardening centers' mailing lists to be updated on sales and to take advantage of any loyalty program promotions. Some hardware and gardening stores offer a guarantee on plants. Always find out the guarantee and exchange program your store offers. Usually, you will need to keep the pots they came in and the receipts. Last season my friend bought some plants that didn't thrive, and she was able to return them for full price by digging them up and putting them back into the pot she bought them in.

April

April showers bring much more than just May flowers. This month boasts some exceptional deals on everything from travel to trees.

- **Summer airfare:** Just two months shy of summer, it's time to get serious about booking your airfare if you plan on taking a vacation this year. Cheapair.com studied nearly 3 million trip itineraries to determine when the best time to buy is. They examined the lowest fare offered for each itinerary every day starting 320 days out. The results: there is no magic number but past studies have pinpointed 54 days as your best bet. And that usually falls starting in April for most summer travel.

- **Vacuums:** Spring cleaning is in full force by now. Vacuums can be a big-ticket purchase with models ranging from $50 to more than $1,000. Do your homework to find the best vacuum in your budget. You don't always need all the bells and whistles to get the job done. And not all homes have the same needs. If you have stairs, you're probably going to want a lightweight vacuum. If you have allergies, consider one with a HEPA filter. Shedding pets may require a vacuum with more power and a special pet-hair attachment. Keep in mind the cost of replacement bags. Canisters that allow you to dump the dirt and reuse may save you money in the long run. For a deep clean, you can rent a steam cleaner. Just be sure to test a small area so you don't damage your carpets. Professional carpet cleaning services will also offer special discounts.

- **Office furniture and free shredding:** With tax season drawing to a close, many people are looking to reorganize and revamp their office life. Now is a good time to find sales on office furniture and supplies. If you plan on cleaning out your file cabinets, check for free shredding events in your area. Many places offer these around Tax Day. Just beware of free shredding limits. Sometimes city governments will team up with waste management facilities to put on free community shredding events. If you can't find one in your area, check for shredding promotions at office supply stores. Or, consider buying your own shredder. They're also likely to go on sale around April 15.

- **Trees:** National Arbor Day always falls on the last Friday of April. Many states observe Arbor Day on different dates, depending on the best time to plant a tree in that particular area. For instance, California celebrates earlier and Maine celebrates later. The key when planting a tree is to do it when weather is mild so roots have time to establish before extreme temperatures arrive. That typically makes spring or fall the best time to plant.

In addition to their beauty and helping to clean the air we breathe; trees have two long-term financial benefits to take into consideration. A mature tree may add resale value to your home. It also can save you money on energy bills. A well-placed tree can shade your home in summer and block winds in winter, saving up to 25% off of a typical home's energy use, according to Energy.gov.

Picking up a tree and planting it yourself is the most budget-friendly strategy if the size is manageable. Paying the extra to have a nursery or landscaper deliver and plant the tree will cost you (sometimes several hundred dollars) but it may give your new tree the best chance at survival. Always check with your gas and electric utility before digging to confirm the area is safe to dig in, even if it's in your own backyard.

May

To me, May is like a breath of fresh air. It's getting warmer, summer is right around the corner, and some great deals will be hitting the stores.

- **Mattresses:** Memorial Day weekend is one of the three times a year you will find significant deals on mattresses. Typically, you don't have to wait until the end of the month to get the deals either. Ask for the store to throw in a free cover or delivery. Make sure they will take your old mattress away. And don't automatically purchase the box spring paired with a mattress in the store. A high-end mattress on a lower-priced box spring or platform usually will work just fine. Most customers might not realize that the posted price can often be negotiated. Some mattress stores sell floor models or returns, always sanitized, at a deep discount. Be sure to ask about their sanitizing procedures. Consider comparing warranties and return/exchange policies. Some stores require you to purchase their water-resistant cover, otherwise you can't return the mattress.

- **Spas:** If you are looking for deals on pampering at a spa, take advantage of packages and discounts the entire month, in honor of Mother's Day. When booking, check to see if slower days and times will mean a deeper discount. Remember: massage schools are a great place to find deals.

- **Everything barbecue:** May is National Barbecue Month, which works beautifully since Memorial Day Weekend is the traditional kick off date for summer and outdoor cooking. This is a great time to get deals on grills and all the accessories. You may be able to find even lower prices in September over Labor Day, but keep in mind the selection may be very limited. Look for perks that go beyond the sale price. Some stores will offer complimentary assembly or to take away your old grill.

- **A fresh coat of paint:** If painting the house is on your to-do list, summer paint sales start with Memorial Day weekend. You can also usually find deals on the other long summer weekends, July 4^{th,} and Labor Day. Don't worry if you're not ready to commit to a color. Ask if you can buy paint that hasn't been tinted yet and come back to have it tinted and shaken, free of charge, when you're ready.

- **Another way to save:** Find out if your paint store sells returned paint or discontinued colors at a discount. If you need to paint a small area, buy a sample size for about $4. Some manufacturers offer rebates so be sure to check with the store or on the manufacturer's website.

- **A stroll through a garden:** Kicking off Mother's Day weekend is National Public Gardens Day, highlighting the beauty of public gardens. Many gardens offer special events and celebrations for the entire family during this time.

June

As the weather heats up in June, so do the deals.

- **Go fish!** National Fishing and Boating Week takes place in June. Look for places in your area where you can fish for free. In some states, free fishing events and dates extend past June. You can also learn tips from the pros with a variety of how-to classes.

- **Movies for the kids:** I remember as a kid hitting the Granada movie theater for a double feature. I felt like it was such deal: two movies for the price of one. If you have children in your life you can still find the deals. Search larger movie chains for summer movie clubs or other bundle offers. In the past while reporting on these packages I was able to find bundles for as little as $5 for 10 movies or $1 movie day at the box office.

- **Tools and home improvement materials:** In honor of Father's Day, you can find significant deals on just about everything in the world of home improvement and tools. Sometimes the deal comes in the form of a bonus gift with purchase. The next time you might see deals this good is Black Friday. A fun addition to the gift: attend one of the store's how-to classes with Dad. Most home improvement stores offer DIY classes on a variety of projects both in-store and virtually. By doing this you are also giving the gift of spending time together.

Home improvement stores usually have a great price adjustment policy. This means if you buy something that goes down in price, usually within a 14-day period, they will give you the difference between what you paid and the lower price back. Home improvement stores are also known for good price matching policies.

July

The July 4th weekend has long been one of the best times of year to score deals. Over the years, those deals have spread throughout the entire month, making July an excellent time to save. Whether you are looking for fun things to do or putting together a new wardrobe, July is a great time to steal the deals.

- **Swimwear:** July is a great time to buy swimwear. Stores need to begin clearing out summer clothes to make room for back to school. You will still be able to find great deals on swimwear and gear in August and September, but design and size selection will be limited.

- **Sunscreen:** July and August are peak sun season which means it's time to stock up on sunscreen. You will find hot deals on a range of sunscreen products and self-tanners. Discounts on sunscreen will continue throughout the end of August. Look for sunscreens that protect against both UVA and UVB radiation.

- **Gym memberships:** Over the summer, gyms begin to empty out as people go on vacation or enjoy the great outdoors. Many clubs offer summer promotions in an effort to increase memberships. It's always a good idea to follow the "try before you buy" rule. Most gyms offer a one-week, no-commitment pass. Another tip: visit the facility during the hours you plan on working out so you will have a better idea of how crowded the gym will be when you plan on being there.

- **Refrigerators and dishwashers:** New models are usually introduced in the spring and summer months. In July, stores will lower prices on prior year models. To continue the savings throughout the year, checkout Energy Star-rated appliances. Find out if your gas and electric company offers credits and rebates for replacing your older refrigerator.

- **Roofing:** Even though winter rain is the furthest thing from our minds, if you have a leaky roof, this is the time to make those repairs. The materials used for roof repair and siding for your home will be on sale throughout July.

- **Free summer concerts:** I am always amazed at the quality of music offered at local summer concert days. Check with your local parks and recreation departments or chamber of commerce to get a list of upcoming free concerts.

   And before you buy a ticket to any concerts, see if your credit card company is offering VIP perks such as preferred seating. Some credit card reward programs will actually allow you to use points to buy your tickets.

August

This month as we savor the last days of summer, we can also savor some significant savings. From wine and bikes to office supplies and eye exams, August does not disappoint.

- **Office supplies:** You don't have to be going back to school to take advantage of the deep discounts office supply stores will be offering. I always stock up on everything I need for my office in August. You'll find deals on notebooks, printer paper, pens, and markers. You can also find deals on high end items like computers and desk chairs. Check back weekly as sales may change. Many of the larger office supply stores offer teacher discounts and rewards, so be sure to ask. Even Apple offers an educational and student discount on a range of items, including Apple Care.

• **Share the deals:** Taking advantage of these office supply sales also is a great way to give back. It's not hard to supply a whole kindergarten class with markers and crayons, when they are selling for less than a dollar a box.

• **Tax-Free Weekends:** August is also the month when many states offer tax-free weekends. This is when back-to-school items, including clothes, shoes, supplies, and even electronics may be tax-free. Check out the Federation of Tax Administrators and Sales Tax Institute to find what is happening in your state.

• **Bikes:** There are a couple times throughout the year that you can find good deals on bicycles and August is one of them. Just like cars, new designs will start coming in around September, so in an effort to make room for new models, stores offer deep discounts starting in August. Unlike cars, the new models often have only minor cosmetic changes keeping the mechanics of the bike the same. This means you can get a prior year's model that may be very similar to the latest design. To save even more, look for floor samples and returned items that come with full warranties.

- **Vino!** Harvest at many vineyards hits at the end of August and that means you can find deals on wine. Check out large liquor stores as well as supermarkets and discount stores for promotions and sales.

- **Eye care:** It's National Eye Exam Month, so there are deals to help you keep your eyes healthy. Check with EyeCare America to see if you qualify for a no-cost eye exam. You might find discounts on eyewear and care through AARP as well. If you live near a college of optometry, you may be able to find really great deals on eye exams.

- **Swimwear:** If you didn't get your swimsuit and summer clothing during the 4th of July sales, it's OK. By the end of this month, prices will be about as low as they go on everything summer. Plus, check for coupon codes and site promos for additional savings.

September

As we say so long to summer, you can say hello to some fantastic September deals. A great month to save, not only because we start the month with Labor Day sales, but many retailers are clearing space for holiday and winter merchandise.

- **Apple products:** Typically, September is when Apple releases their new iPhone models. This means you might find previous generations discounted. If your current phone is in good condition, you may be able to get a credit through Apple's trade-in program or sell it online. Don't forget, Apple offers educational discounts. So, if you are a teacher or student, or you qualify under their educational discount program, you may receive additional savings on products and Apple Care. Parents and students are eligible with a high school or secondary school ID. Teachers discount rates may be different than the student discount rate. Make sure to save all of your receipts and documents if you buy Apple Care.

- **Coupons:** September is National Coupon Month. I've mentioned coupons many times in this book. My parents always clipped coupons but these days not only are coupons available online 24/7 but the range of products offering coupons is limitless. Coupons and coupon codes are one of the easiest ways to save money. In celebration of National Coupon Month, look for higher value coupons. Be sure to join your grocery store and drug store loyalty programs to save even more money.

- **Holiday travel:** Now is the time to book your holiday travel. Not only will you find better deals but you will find a much better selection on flights and seats. Waiting to purchase holiday travel is not recommended, especially if you are traveling to a destination with limited flights. If you have the option to fly out of or into more than one airport, be sure to compare prices. I have found there can be a significant savings just by changing the airport.

- **Luggage:** September is a fantastic time to buy luggage. When shopping for luggage compare warranties in addition to price. And keep in mind that most airlines charge for checked luggage over 50 pounds. So, think lightweight when making your purchase.

- **New cars:** If you have been waiting to buy a new car, your wait is over. September is historically the best month to negotiate a deal on both a new car and a used car. Most dealerships will be clearing their showroom floors to make room for their new models. In addition to offering new model incentives, prior year models will also be on sale. Consider a certified pre-owned car for extra assurance. These are cars that have been inspected and offer a warranty. Don't jump on the first deal you see. September has 30 days and you can usually score the best deals closer to the end of the month. Shop weekdays rather than on the weekends when the showrooms are busier. You want a salesperson to have the time to answer all of your questions and negotiate with you.

- **Outdoor living:** Almost everything you can imagine for your outdoor living space will be marked down starting with Labor Day sales. Patio furniture, grills, outdoor rugs, and more will be drastically reduced in September. One thing I do when I need to make a larger purchase like an appliance or patio furniture is to check my credit card points balance. I accumulate a lot of points from using my credit card and I can trade in those points for a wide range of store gift cards. So, not only do I get the sale price but I can use gift cards to help with the purchase.

October

Truth be told, October is filled with some bargains that may even top the busiest shopping month of November. Here are some of the best deals you'll find this month.

- **Toys:** October is a huge month for toy clearance because stores are making shelf space for the holiday inventory. There are still some great finds even though not all will make the Top 10 Toy List. By the first of the month most stores have released their layaway programs, so make sure to sign up soon if you plan to use them. If Santa decides to wait to shop for your toys the week before Christmas, there is a chance he will need to give you an IOU instead.

- **Kids' clothes:** Post-back-to-school sales often occur now to make way for holiday merchandise.

- **Nuts:** Nut harvest mostly occurs around this time, especially for almonds, pecans and walnuts. National Nut Day is on Oct. 22, so keep an eye out for special promotions around that time.

- **Shrubs and trees:** Nurseries are pushing their warm weather stock out the door with big sales. Not everything sold at this time will survive the cold winter months, but shrubs and trees are often a good, sustainable choice that are still on sale.

- **Halloween costumes**: If you procrastinate and wait until the last minute, you'll find some heavily discounted Halloween costumes, but only a very limited selection. Instead, do your costume shopping at consignment and resale stores. Many of these locations stock up for the month, and provide discounts of 50% to 85% off the original retail price. And since Halloween costumes are usually worn just once, you can find "just like new" costumes at bargain prices. There are other smart options including Goodwill or the Salvation Army, which are perfect vendors for DIY Halloween costume supplies. Start early for the best selection.

- **Pink products**: October is also Breast Cancer Awareness Month, which means pink products are lining the shelves. It can be a win-win since a percentage of your purchase will go to charity. Be sure to keep an eye out for reduced-cost mammogram and breast exam events. You can contact your local hospital to find out what services they will be offering.

November

This is the time of year when extra expenses creep into our monthly budget. Between increased energy bills, holiday travel, and gifts we can easily spend an extra $1,000 or more before the end of the year. Fortunately, November will also bring along big sales like Black Friday and Cyber Monday.

- **Medical insurance:** From about Nov. 1 until Dec. 15 you can shop for new medical coverage and make any changes to your current medical insurance plan. Start early because the process, known as Open Enrollment, can take some time.

You can go to HealthCare.gov to search for plans in your state. Really do your homework. Make sure to compare the deductibles and coverage each plan offers. We have much more about this in my chapter on medical expenses.

- **Military and Veteran's Day deals:** In honor of Veteran's Day, veterans and military personnel can get additional deals on everything from car washes to free meals. Sites like Militarybenefits.info and Military.com help you navigate what deals are offered.

- **Television sets:** Historically, electronics are a big-ticket item at a low price on Black Friday. Just be certain there is a written warranty included.

- **Home improvement:** If you have been thinking of painting or remodeling, now may be the time. Contractors, handymen, and painters have slower schedules this time of the year, which can translate into discounts for you. Make sure you check a contractor's license before you begin working with them. If you are remodeling a kitchen or bathroom, you can often save money if you purchase the appliance and fixtures on your own. This way you can find the best deal, use any additional discounts, and have the items delivered.

- **Tools:** That's right, tools are a bargain on Black Friday. Not only will you find deals but many manufacturers will offer a bonus with purchase.

- **Baking supplies:** Since Thanksgiving is the traditional start of the holiday baking season, baking supplies and ingredients will be going on sale at the beginning of November. If a sale item is out of stock, ask for a raincheck. This will allow you to get the item at the sale price when it is back in stock, even if it's no longer on sale.

- **Perfume and cosmetics**: November and December are great months to find gifts with the purchase of cosmetics and fragrances. Stock up on what you need now to take advantage of all the freebies. That's what I do.

- **Price adjustments:** I always recommend saving your receipts for a potential price adjustment. This is especially important this time of the year when items will continuously be dropping in price as the holidays approach. Many stores, especially larger department stores, will give you a period of time to get money back if the item you purchase goes down in price. Basically, the difference between what you paid and the new sale price would be credited back to you. The usual price adjustment period is 10 to 14 days. So, mark your calendars to check back with the store. Usually you just need to bring in the receipt, not the merchandise, to get the adjustment.

December

The minute Black Friday hits, shoppers are in full swing shopping mode. Most of us shop more in December than any other month of the year. Between gifts, parties, food, spirits, and travel we tend to spend in December. Fortunately, you will find deals on just about everything this month and, of course, there are a few items that are extra special best buys for December.

- **Electronic bundles:** Electronics are a hot buy between Black Friday and Christmas Day. To get an even better deal, look for stores offering a bundle: extra items that are added onto your electronics purchase. For example, video games are often bundled with gaming systems. You may find laptop purchases bundled with gift cards. Bundles are the secret to turning your electronics purchase into a December best buy. You will see more bundled deals around the holidays than any other time of the year. By waiting until the last week of December or right after the New Year, you may score even better deals. Stores will be flooded with returns and often, if the item isn't in the original packaging, it is sold as an open-box, meaning additional discounts for you. Make sure that you save the original packaging from these purchases. Some products cannot be returned without the original packaging, others may not be returned if they are opened, so make sure to check the store policy.

- **Outlet shopping:** Outlet malls have become a go-to spot for shoppers to find deals. December deals won't disappoint with stores adding additional markdowns to already low prices. Most outlet malls will have a customer service office. You want to start your shopping trip there and ask about AARP, AAA, military, and student discounts. Some outlet malls will give you a mall discount coupon just for checking in.

- **Clothing:** The day after Christmas and New Year's Day are two of the best days to get deals on clothing. Expect to see sales of up to 75% off. Add to that any store coupons you may have. Larger department stores will typically send out coupons to cardholders for additional discounts if you spend a certain amount. Most of the deals will be for winter clothes like coats, sweaters, and flannel. Not to worry. There are plenty of cold months still ahead.

15. HOW TO GET CUSTOMER SERVICE

*"It shouldn't require consumers going to TV stations
to have their rights properly addressed."*

California Congresswoman Jackie Speier

These words stuck with me as Sen. Jackie Speier addressed fellow committee members of the California Senate in 2006. I was listening to testimony at the capitol because I had been investigating certain business practices of the wireless industry and had brought the story to then California Senator Speier. Our consumer team at CBS in San Francisco had already been working on it for several years. The senator had sponsored a bill to protect the rights of consumers who were faced with unauthorized charges when their cell phones were stolen. The bill passed committee that day and would eventually make it to the desk of then Gov. Arnold Schwarzenegger, where unfortunately it was vetoed. As I listened to her speak, I realized that unfortunately it often does take media involvement to push companies to do the right thing. I can't tell you how many times I have called a business on behalf of a viewer who was getting nowhere with resolving an issue and then suddenly, almost magically, the problem went away when I called. But Speier was right, it shouldn't have to take a TV station to help consumers resolve their problems with companies.

This particular series of stories was titled *The Wireless Runaround*. It all started when a young woman wrote to me about being charged thousands of dollars for unauthorized calls made from her stolen cell phone. After we aired her story, the floodgates opened. We received so many more letters from people facing the same issue. We went on to do nearly two dozen stories and two primetime specials. When we brought our findings to the state attorney general's office, finally, positive change started happening. Based on our investigative findings, consumers were refunded charges they paid that they were not responsible for, wording on contracts was revised, and fines were issued. My team and I really felt our work paid off. We were honored with several journalism awards, but the best part was it was a big win for consumers.

Nowadays, when good customer service is largely a thing of the past, it's hard for individual consumers to be heard, and it can take the power of the media to get a company's attention. But there *are* things that you can do to on your own that will make it more likely you will have success.

How to Get to a Resolution

I have been there and I get it. Navigating a customer service hotline is often an exercise in frustration. From the moment you pick up your phone and dial that toll-free number, you often feel this will be nothing but a waste of time. I will admit there have been many times I have been on hold and just started frantically pushing buttons and totally lose patience to the point where I am yelling! This behavior usually kicks in at around the 15-minutes-or-more wait-time mark. To add to the frustration, once I connect to a real person, I'm often told I need to be connected to another department and to "please hold."

If you are wondering if it is easier to just live with the consumer problem than try to get it resolved, I will tell you it is worth it to try to fix it. By handling issues like overcharges or unfair fees you will be keeping the money in your pocket which is where you want it to be. One of the most important things to do is find a way to connect with an actual human being instead of a machine.

GetHuman.com is a helpful website that catalogs direct-to-human representative numbers for a range of popular companies. This allows you to bypass automated systems that usually lead you to extended wait times and button pressing. If you can't find a number listed on Gethuman.com, you can also try the old-fashioned way of just pressing '0' to see if you are connected to an operator or representative right away.

Be Prepared. Write it Down

Before calling a company for help, make sure to have a detailed list of your concerns and problems in front of you. Write out a script articulating what you expect the company to do for you. If applicable, include examples of any attempts to solve the issue on your own. Being as thorough and specific as possible will help the representative do their job. It will also help avoid wasting time going over potential solutions you tried but didn't work. Your representative may appreciate your effort and may go to greater lengths to help you.

Throughout the conversation, take detailed notes. Be sure to note the date, time, your representative's name, ID number, and any reference or confirmation numbers. This can be helpful later on down the line if another problem arises and you want to be directed to the specific person that helped you or if you need to reference what was discussed. If you come to a resolution, ask for a confirmation email or letter. If they can't provide you with this, ask for their email to send them a confirmation. You can be persistent while still being polite. Kindness always counts. If you get someone who is difficult, you can end the call and try again. Chances are you will be connected with someone new. I've done this more than once and gotten help the second time around.

Don't Take No for an Answer

Never be afraid to ask for a supervisor if you feel you are not getting the proper assistance. If you don't get your desired resolution, writing a letter to the CEO or president of the company may help. If you decide to do that, make it about your problem, your frustration, and let them know you would like to continue using their product/service. Offer constructive criticism rather than ranting about how awful their company is. You would be amazed how helpful this can be. I did this once for a service I was using for my dog, Puccini. After about nine calls and getting no resolution, I wrote a letter to the CEO. I explained what happened and the bind I was left in but I also expressed how much I value a service like theirs. The CEO and two people from their customer service team scheduled a call to learn more about not only what happened, but we discussed ways to improve their customer experience. They truly cared about their customers and wanted to grow. In the end, we had a very productive call and as a thank you for my time and for my inconveniences they sent me a generous gift card. I wasn't expecting that but it was surely appreciated.

Consumer Complaints

3,000,000. That is the number of consumer complaints the Federal Trade Commission (FTC) received in its last reporting year, as I write this book. And that is just what was reported! Scams, ID theft, and debt collectors top the list of complaints to the FTC. Identity theft complaints are so high, the FTC has set up a website, IdentityTheft.gov, so consumers can file reports and develop a recovery plan from identity theft.

One of the challenges for consumers is finding the correct agency or resource to help solve a complaint. To help take the guess work out of this daunting task, ConsumerAction.org has designed a Consumer Services Guide. This searchable database of agencies and resources helps consumers solve their complaints as well as learn about groups and agencies that work on behalf of consumers. Categories range from legal assistance and utilities, to travel and fitness. The guide is very user-friendly with solid resources to point you in the right direction. They also have a free, useful library of publications.

If in the end you are getting no resolution for your issue, the power of the media shining a light on a serious unresolved problem can do wonders. We received thousands of calls and letters every year from consumers with complaints. I have seen and heard just about everything from everyone. The stories and their battles were often outrageous.

We were able to help resolve many problems that never made it onto TV. But some of these issues became TV news stories. In fact, my best stories were from viewers who had hit a wall, knew they had rights, but could not make their voices heard. Other important stories involved businesses causing people harm. I do realize that the battle of getting a consumer complaint not only heard but actually resolved feels like the story of David and Goliath. But if you feel like David, know that you have resources, agencies, and advocacy groups out there to help you against almost any Goliath.

Customer Service Cheat Sheet

- **Keep detailed records:** I have a special notebook that I use for ongoing issues. It has pockets in the side so that I can easily save copies of bills or photos of products. Write down each date that you attempt to contact the company and summarize what happened and how much time you spent on it.

- **Try to connect with a human:** GetHuman.com lists customer service numbers to various companies. You can also hit "0" when prompted by the robo-operator.

- **Know your warranty inside-out:** If you have a warranty for a service or product you are calling about, have all of the information handy. If it is a recent purchase using a credit card, see if there was additional coverage provided by using that card.

- **Have your credit card company step in:** If you have a dispute, you can open an inquiry with the credit card you used. They will research the dispute and possibly reverse the charges.

- **Don't take no for an answer:** Be prepared to ask for a supervisor if you can't get your issue resolved. If all else fails, write a letter to the CEO of the company.

- **Manners matter:** Despite the frustration level, remember to keep your cool. You will find it's worth it in the long run.

16. LET'S DO THIS

Helping You

This book really was built on a lifetime of lessons: those I learned from my parents, those I learned the hard way, those I learned as a reporter interviewing experts, and those I learned from people I interviewed as they overcame challenges. If you apply the tips I've shared in these pages to your own life, you should see a significant improvement in your ability to save. If you apply a few tips, you will see a few improvements. What you put into it is what you will get out of it. There is no right or wrong way. Just know that there's always a better way to save and saving can lead to joy.

Help Yourself

One of my favorite sayings is: Knowledge is power. I have always tried to educate myself, viewers, and readers with a toolbox of empowering information. You now have a very large set of tools to build a strong foundation for your financial house, a house you can live in and enjoy. Make the choice to have fun while applying these tips to your life. If you take away nothing else from this book, know this: You have the power to create a different story. It may start in your mind, but with persistence and faith, your dreams can become your reality.

So You Can Help Others

While writing this book, I wanted to create a community of people dedicated to helping themselves *and* helping others. There is great value in helping others and the rewards are priceless. I have volunteered for most of my life for causes that are close to my heart. Both of my parents lived their lives giving back. Some of the things they did were small, like my mom helping price items at the Catholic Charities thrift shop or making Christmas ornaments for the church boutique. My dad joined the Lions Club as a young man. The Lions describe themselves as "1.4 million people who believe kindness matters." When he passed away, he was one of the oldest Lions at the age of 91.

I remember while growing up my parents put $2 in the church collection every Sunday and $5 on holidays. I did a story where I interviewed my dad about the importance of helping others and he said, "It's not that you have to take money out of your pocket, especially if you don't have it. But the energy that you put forward in doing all of these endeavors pays off in the long run. Give time, because time will generate funds from other sources. Give without worrying about what you're going to get back."

When he was nearing the end of his life, I asked my father what quote meant the most to him so that I could put it on the cover of a little book I was creating: *The Book of Galdoisms.* He showed me his version of a quote by French-American Quaker missionary Etienne de Grellet that he had typed out on a little piece of paper in 1945.

> *"I shall pass through this world but once. Any good thing therefore that I can do or any kindness that I can show to any human being, let me do it now. Let me not defer or neglect it, for I shall not pass this way again."*

This quote sums up my feelings about this book. We have one life to live, but we have many opportunities to create and recreate that life. And this includes our finances. We may *'pass thru this world'* once, but every second of the day we have a choice as to how we pass through. As for goodness and kindness, start by showing both to yourself first and then to others. By strengthening others, we strengthen ourselves. I hope this book helped you to help yourself as you continue on your journey. And as this final quote says, *"Let me do it now. Let me not defer or neglect it, for I shall not pass this way again."* So, let's do this! We are all in this together.

A HEARTFELT THANKS

"Nice having you. Thank you!" I heard from a friendly voice atop a winding staircase outside the control room of our local NBC station. This was 1998 and I had been invited to do a money saving segment for the morning news. The voice was the senior producer, Christina Ricci. Little did I know at that moment I was meeting a woman who would become one of my producers at CBS 5, a producer and collaborator for many future projects, and most importantly my dear friend. When I started writing this book, she was the first person I called to help with this undertaking. Her passion, brilliance, insight, and wit have helped fill these pages. Christina, having you along for this ride has meant the world to me. I am forever grateful.

Over 20 years in TV you get to work with hundreds of producers and I have been fortunate to work with some of the best. I thank all of them for their guidance and giving me opportunities. I am especially grateful to Andrew Shinnick, Jeff Harris, Sandy Lee, Craig Franklin, Josh Zerkel, Susan Sullivan, Steve Fyffe, Rick Villaroman, Shirley Davalos, Tom Spitz, Dan Rosenheim, and Ed Nieto.

Seth Isler, thank you for your brilliant research and for creating a series of TV segments with my father. He loved being your star!

Dianne Luby-Lane, Sam Anagnostou, Brad Bostick, Ned Colletti, Candi Athens, Julie Baumann, Tami Ciligriano, Nancy Hayes, Karyn Bradley, and Sarah Symons, thank you for your friendship over the years.

Anne Stanley and Dave Calloway, thank you for the opportunities to be a columnist for some of the top financial news outlets. You have both played such an important part in helping me to help others.

Felix, who had no idea I was writing a book, told me, "Your dad is saying to finish your book. He will help you from the other side." Thanks for the message!

Sister Rita Marie Brown, thank you for telling me, after my constant detentions for talking in class, "Ms. Pavini, we are going to make that voice of yours work to your advantage." You ignited in me the love of writing, speaking, and storytelling as you coached me to become a competitive student speaker.

I have been blessed with two amazing families that have been brought together as one. Thanks to Mike for being an amazing big brother with the biggest heart. Madeline and Michael, for always being so supportive and kind to me. My brother Jim who is a hero in every sense of the word. And to my Musci family by marriage, thank you for your open arms and hearts. Adrienne, thanks for always being on the other end of the phone for me with your humor and wisdom. All of you, both here and on the other side, mean so much to me and I thank you for always showing me unconditional love.

Tom, you are not only the best husband but truly my best friend. Thanks for always having my back. Paloma and Brandon you add so much to our lives. Paloma, thanks for your insight on chapter after chapter. And Puccini Pavini, my loyal dog, thanks for curling up next to me while I typed for hours on end.

To the thousands of viewers and readers over the years who have shared their personal struggles, challenges, and successes in an effort to help the greater good, it has been my privilege to tell your stories.

Lastly, Dad and Mom, to say thank you for all you have done for me seems like a vast understatement...but gratefully and humbly, thank you.

BIOGRAPHY

Jeanette Pavini is a multi-award-winning consumer and investigative reporter. As a native San Franciscan, her career began in the Bay Area at the local NBC station before a decade as the chief consumer reporter for CBS 5. She has been a featured guest contributor on the *Today Show* and shares her advice with hundreds of media outlets including *Good Morning America*, *The Wall Street Journal Digital Network* and *Oprah.com*. Jeanette worked as the personal finance contributor to the *Hallmark Home & Family Show* and *The Better Show* as well as a special reports contributor to the *USA Today* video network. As a columnist for *The Wall Street Journal Sunday*, *Better Homes & Gardens*, *AARP*, *TheStreet.com*, and *MarketWatch*, her advice gives readers unique strategies to save money, protect themselves as consumers, and find joy in saving.

Jeanette is the recipient of two Emmy Awards, seven Emmy nominations, The Edward R. Murrow Award, The Associated Press Award, two National Headliner Awards, and nine Press Club Awards. She was voted among the best personal finance experts in the U.S., in GoBankingRates.com's competition. She is the recipient of the prestigious National Consumer Action Award in Media for her work as a consumer advocate. In 2014, Jeanette was honored at the United States House of Representatives in Washington D.C. with the Gold Star Wives Award of Excellence for her in-depth series and work to bring attention to military widows being denied benefits. Her three-year investigation into the wireless industry's business practices led to the first of its kind settlement with the Attorney General's Office, which gave millions of dollars back to Californians. Her investigation aired on *30 Minutes* (created by Don Hewitt) and two primetime specials. In 2011, she wrote and produced her first documentary, *From Hell to Heaven* which focused on the dedicated people working for change in the world of human trafficking.

Jeanette is the co-author of *Raising Baby Green* (Jossey-Bass), the recipient of the Nautilus Gold Medal Book Award. She is on the board for Her Future Coalition and the emeritus board for the Crohn's & Colitis Foundation. Jeanette works nationally but her home and heart are in San Francisco. Follow her on social media and sign up for her *Joy of Saving Secrets* by going to JeanettePavini.com.

Galdo kept his ledgers, notebooks, envelope system, and his volunteer work with the Lions Club going until July 8, 2015. He went up to help organize the books in Heaven, four days later, on July 12, 2015.

Made in USA - Kendallville, IN
1213631_9781098341770
12.28.2020 1239